A portion of the proceeds from this book will
be used to send kids with disabilities to
Young Life Capernaum camps.

"Marilyn and I have been friends and Young Life colleagues with John and Gae Wagner for over twenty years. We have watched them learn the lessons and gain the insights that John shares in this book. He tells the truth. He is authentic and honest and helpful in what he writes. I encourage you to enter the Wagners' world!"

—Denny Rydberg,
President, Young Life

"Irresistibly compelling & bracingly honest, this isn't a book to devour in a hurry. Read it slowly...savor the stories... experience the difference between believing that God is love and experiencing the love of God. *Perfect* will lead you into the heart of God, which is the finest recommendation I could give any book."

—Fil Anderson,
Executive director, Journey Resources, author of *Running on Empty: Contemplative Spirituality for Overachievers*

"Watching John's relationship with his son David is a window into the life with God I long for. *Perfect* will introduce you to the outlandishness of God's love in the midst of profound challenge. John's reflections on life with God, through his life with David avoid sentimentalizing piety and cynical acquiescence. The joy of this father and son relationship inspires me to hope beyond hope."

—Jason Gaboury O.P.,
Regional Director NY/NJ, Intervarsity Collegiate Ministries

"For all of David's life I have had the opportunity to watch John and Gae parent him. You see in spring of 2000, when David was a baby, John invited me to join the Young Life staff with the goal that there be Young Life for David, and other kids like him, by the time David would be a teenager. John's desire for David to experience God's love has motivated him to take huge risks, to advocate hard for kids that were being overlooked, and to dive deep into God's love himself. As with most things with God, the journey has been different than expected; the lows have been very low, but the highs have been amazingly miraculous. Through it all, John will let you know that he has seen God clearly and come to know God better through life with David. And the good news is—the joy, the smiles, the delight, and the dancing are not over yet!"

—Pam Harmon,
Vice President of Young Life Capernaum

"When God transforms the heart of a man through the precious gift of a most remarkable son, that father has something pretty profound to say to us all. That's John Wagner in his new work, *Perfect*—you'll be deeply blessed by his stories, insights, and practical encouragements. I heartily recommend this small but significant book you hold in your hands!"

—Joni Eareckson Tada,
Joni and Friends International Disability Center

"Vibrant. Beautiful. John Wagner's transparent stories of his precious relationship with his son David welcome us right into their midst. The book is a dynamic love letter inviting us to participate in the unbridled hope and possibilities of life lived fully and well. John's winsome way makes us want to be part of his story—and then we see that we are. Powerful. Clear."

—John Featherston
Senior Director, New Ventures at Chick-fil-A, Inc.

"I have known John Wagner since he was a fresh-faced Wake Forest graduate who moved to our neighborhood in Washington DC to hang out with teenagers. John is the real deal. He is passionate about grabbing kids with the good news that Jesus loves them unconditionally. In *Perfect: Sacred Stories from the Heart of a Dad*, John shares what his youngest son David has taught his family, and all of us, about God's joyous, contagious love. This book will melt your heart with a fresh perspective on our Father's abundant grace amidst life's valleys and mountains."

—Dennis Bakke,
Author of *Joy at Work*
Co-Founder and Chancellor, Imagine Schools

"This is an incredibly moving devotional written by an overachieving father who learns how to receive everything he was trying to earn. And his teacher is his son who has Down Syndrome. I was one of the Wagner's pastors when David was born. I remember praying that his family would find him to be a grace from God. Clearly, that is exactly who David has been. This book reveals how those with a disability have the extraordinary ability to show us what it means to be fully alive. Read it slowly, and keep the tissues nearby."

—Dr. Craig Barnes
President, Princeton Theological Seminary

"In brilliant form, *Perfect* captures the essence of life with Jesus—through the experience of parenting a special child. John's vulnerability is a gift to each of us, helping us redefine God's ideals and discover a father's unconditional love for his children."

—Gabe Lyons.
Author, *The Next Christians* and Founder of Q

"These insights run deep and come from a place of vulnerability that is life giving to all who dare to take them in. Life takes on a new dimension when you can't hide or pretend, and when you dare to no longer make excuses. But it is so liberating when you have eyes to see what so many of us miss every day simply because we hide, pretend and make excuses. Within these pages you'll be invited to a new place, a place of freedom and hope. A place that a special relationship between a Father and his one of a kind son have to offer. Get ready to laugh, cry, hope and be challenged."

—Pat Goodman,
Director of Men's Ministry, Grace Fellowship Church, Young Life National Training Consultant

"At first, this powerful memoir of raising a special needs child will strike you as the inspiring story of how someone else has risen to life's challenges. Then it will challenge you to explore deeply what it means to love and be loved, to trust and be trusted, and to face your own struggles with joy. With honesty, humility and humor, John Wagner has written a testimony that perfectly integrates Scripture and life experience. *Perfect* shows us what it means to live an imperfect life rooted and grounded in love."

—Rev. Donna Marsh
Associate Pastor, National Presbyterian Church

"I've spent years interviewing remarkable people--people who have amazing lives or incredible talent or stunning luck. I'm not sure any of them could reflect as deeply, or as amusingly, as John Wagner has on what their experiences have illuminated about living, relationships and faith. To many people, David would seem like a burden. John has proved he's a blessing. This book just pulses with joy, wisdom, hope and funny stories. (If you hate the way you laugh, you might want to read chapter 14 in a solitary place.)"

—Belinda Luscombe,
Editor at large, TIME magazine.

"In *Perfect* David and John encourage us to live more authentically from our hearts. A "look no hands" joy ride through the ups and downs of life that lands you smack dab in the loving arms of God."

–Chuck Millsaps,
President, Great Outdoor Provision Co.

"When I was in college, I took a course on the original indigenous peoples of America. Many of the groups elevated those with mental or physical disabilities to the highest status, as "gods who lived among them", because they possessed supernatural, divine-like attributes. John captures these realities present in his son David, while at the same time, encourages us to grow into them, with the help of Jesus and the power of the Holy Spirit. This isn't your normal devotional, happily so. It is fun, honest, and deep."

–Ty Saltzgiver,
Author of *My First Thirty Quiet Times*

"David's life is an incredible gift to his father, and John Wagner describes the life-transforming lessons he has learned through David, with such poignancy and joy. Through David, John has learned about the unconditional love of God for all. As their pastor, I have seen David's irrepressible spirit making him leap up in dance to the music in worship, and John's unabashed joining in the dance. John's journey with David--moving, ebullient, peppered with marks of God's grace, is written with humor, thoughtfulness and such joy."

–Rev. Milind Sojwal,
Rector, All Angels Episcopal Church, New York City

"I just finished reading this amazing book cover to cover. It is a love story between a dad and his son who becomes his mentor. A young man whom the world considers a tough luck case. John Wagner takes us on a journey of what's under the veil. Jesus himself disguised as his son. Read, laugh, cry, wonder and be changed. And find out about how a wild crazy God reveals himself precisely and most powerfully through John's son. I am happy for you if you just picked this book up to read."

—Nick Palermo,
Founder of Young Life's Capernaum Ministries, Author of *Missing Stars, Fallen Sparrows*

Perfect:
Sacred Stories from the
Heart of a Dad
by John T. Wagner

© Copyright 2015 John Wagner

ISBN 978-1-63393-198-5

Published by

◄ köehlerbooks™

210 60th Street
Virginia Beach, VA 23451
212-574-7939
www.koehlerbooks.com

Perfect:

SACRED STORIES FROM
THE HEART OF A DAD

John T. Wagner

VIRGINIA BEACH
CAPE CHARLES

Dedication

To Michael and Jessi, who have loved David and me so well and who have shared in all of our family's sacred stories. I love you both, and in both of you, I am well pleased.

"But God chose the foolish things of the world to shame the wise; God chose the weak things of this world to shame the strong."

—Apostle Paul

Table of Contents

Introduction

Gae and I were driving to North Carolina to see my brother and his family. We were somewhere between Durham and Greensboro on I-40, driving sleepily along with our two beautiful kids, a boy and a girl, our cute little dog, and our fairly new, recently purchased mid-sized minivan, me with my gorgeous, blond Texan wife, she with me, and "Hootie" cranking on the cassette, hurtling down the road towards Asheville, NC. I had just been promoted at work, we had bought a nice brick, four-bedroom, hardwood-floor, working-fireplace, big-back-porch house set in the city with a yard and room for a swing. Ministry was booming. We loved our church. Life was good, real good, almost perfect. Why mess that up? We're good. Check. Check. Check. Done.

The year was 1995.

Gae and I had had this conversation before. For those of you who are married, you realize the importance of timing. Some things need to wait, to marinate. Other things, you just need to move on. It had been maybe six months since I had brought this up. It went nowhere. Complete dud. I had dropped it. Figured we just weren't ready.

But this day felt different. I felt good. I felt lucky. I felt some movement. Connected. Oneness. Positive. Sense of direction. Mojo. Maybe God was truly with me this time. Maybe stars were aligning. Maybe I had some flow that wasn't with me the last time

So I did. I just blurted it out. "What do you think about having another kid, a baby?" There it was. As a guy and an extravert, I am uncomfortable with silence. I look to fill the air. I want to keep talking, explain myself, see different sides and angles, perspectives. Work on a timeline. Problem solve. I did none of that. I just let it out and let it lay there. Like a big egg. And waited.

"I'd be open to that," she said.

"Huh? What? What did you say?" I almost wrecked the car. Our lives are perfect. Why would we want to mess that up? Why would we want another kid? We have two, one of each—they are gorgeous, perfect. We are just hitting our stride. We have momentum. Life is good, real good.

I won't bore you with the details, but it took us over two years to get pregnant. We had one miscarriage and some complications in between. But then, one day in early September, that little pink stick turned blue, or the little blue stick turned pink, or whatever it does, and Gae looked at me and said, "I'm pregnant." And we laughed, we cried, we hugged, we held hands. We were good. We were happy. We were nervous, but we were happy.

Preparations for a third child are not like preparations for a first child. We had the crib and baby carrier, "the Graco," which was the portable crib (I would say, without any real exaggeration, that I probably set up and took down that thing maybe 10,000 times over the life of our kids. I got to a point where I could do it in less than three seconds, starting with it wrapped in its case, in the dark with two crying babies, one under each arm, a diaper in my back pocket, and a bottle under my chin), the car seat, the baby books, clothes, bottles, diapers, b-pump, stroller, and you name it. We were set. Kid was even going to have his own room, which had never happened in our house.

So we did what you do when you're pregnant—we waited. We talked about names. We looked at little-kid clothes. Technology had changed quite a bit since Jessi was born, so we got sonograms that looked like photographs and shared them with friends and family. Everyone thought they were great and "cute." We were so excited. We laughed with our kids, read them stories, and talked about their little baby brother or, if God was unusually kind, a sister.

Gae had said later that things "had felt a little different." But they didn't feel different to me. We had one sonogram where the doctor said, "We are a little concerned that his legs are short and his head is large." Then he looked at me and laughed. "Nevermind. Chip off the old block. You guys are good. Enjoy, Big Head."

The day we went to the hospital, we were both giggling and laughing. Gae was in a little pain, but we had the windows down, radio on, and it was a beautiful spring day. We were doing it man, feeling and looking good. I walked into the hospital like I had just won the World Series. "Hey, what's happening? I know, 'bout to have a baby. How you feelin'?" Talking to the nurses, getting checked in, texting, and giving a couple of high fives, maybe a double finger gun or two, and then I headed up to the room.

Looked like the same room Michael and Jessi were born in—3rd floor, Columbia Hospital for Women—25th and Lst NW in DC. Our midwife had just shown up. Gae was in labor. You could see the Washington Monument out our window. If the Nats were in DC at the time, they would have been in town. My parents were with our kids—they were happy. Everyone was happy. All our friends were waiting to hear the news. They were happy.

And then it broke. Our world split apart. Crashed. Car wreck. Splintered. Broken. Shattered. Speechless. Crushed. Destroyed. There is not a parent in the world that doesn't remember the first few moments of when they found out their child has disabilities like it was yesterday—the smells, the sounds, the place, the people, what you were wearing, where you were, who was speaking.

We didn't call anyone. We didn't talk to anyone. No one came over. We just sat there and held our baby and held each other. Gae said at one point, "I will raise this child, but I will never be happy again." Our lives were over.

Actually, they were just starting.

As David grew and got older, I realized that God was shaping me and teaching me in ways I had never experienced before. Hardly a day would go by where I wouldn't learn something about me, about life, and about God and Jesus through David—things about joy and peace and rhythm and courage and celebration and gratitude and suffering and surrender and what it means to be cherished and loved. So I started to write those things down and journal through them and wonder about them. And finally Gae said, "I think you need to share that. Somebody else needs to hear that."

So here it is. As best I can do. Some of my favorite stories of David coupled with my favorite stories of Jesus. I've told more than one person, the best part of the whole book are the pictures. So if that's all you do, you've probably done the best part.

This is not everyone's experience, I know that. This is my experience, with my son. It's all I got. I try not to glamorize it or tidy it up. I try to tell it as best I can in all its mess and glory—the good, the bad, the hard, the laughter, the tears.

My hope, the way the book is laid out, is that it would be an experience. No more than one chapter a day, or if you are doing this with a small group, one chapter a session. Take your time. Read the scripture, look at the picture, sit for some time in silence—let it sink in. Listen. Wait. Read the scripture again. Then read the chapter. Wait some more. Laugh, cry, get angry, let God move you, and, above all, engage. God works from the inside out. This is nothing, actually don't even bother, if it isn't transformation. It should change you. Be open to it. Be open to how God wants to use it and speak to you through it.

Take the time to journal, to write, to listen. The questions are intended to simply help you get started, get ideas flowing, open up. If you are leading this with a group, the questions are a place to start. You probably have better ones.

And then pray. And pray out loud. Sing if you need to. Dance. Listen to a song. Praise, thanksgiving, worship. The whole thing should take about an hour. Slow it down.

Relax and enjoy. Perfect.

1

Boogie Boards

"My name is Legion," he replied,
"for we are many" (Mark 5:9).

READ

Psalm 93
Mark 5:1-20

SILENCE.

I have never met a kid that loved the water more than David. As a family we love the ocean. There is something about the rhythm of the waves, the pounding nature, the physicality of being in the surf, the surge of water, the weight—how it wraps itself around you almost like a hug—the constant ebb and flow, the unpredictability, the washing machine-like nature of being tumbled over backwards by a wave—what I often like to call a "slobberknocker"—and somersaulting, head over heels, towards the beach. David absolutely loves it, the rougher the better.

We have friends who live and own places near the beach in St. Augustine, Florida. It has become one of our favorite places to visit, either over a spring break or in the summer. One thing that we realized shortly after we moved to New York is that here they also have a *winter break*, which generally happens the second week of February when it is so cold here you think you moved to the Ukraine.

Two years ago, on our first *winter break*, we went to St. Augustine, to the beach. What we didn't realize is that it was *winter* there as well. We got off the plane, and instead of it being 85 degrees and sunny, which is what we were hoping, it was 55 degrees, cloudy, with a 25 mph wind.

BEACH

That didn't stop David. After unpacking the car and getting settled, we decided to *take a walk on the beach.* We weren't down there fifteen minutes when we look up and he is in the water.

Two things David doesn't have that you would expect most kids his age to have—a temperature gauge on his body that basically says, "If this water gets five degrees colder, it will ice over. The ocean will turn to a massive glacier of ice." Maybe it's the Down syndrome, maybe all the hummus and pasta, but for some reason, David's body is not telling him that.

The other thing he doesn't have is a healthy sense of danger. "These waves are two stories tall. If I go out there now, they will toss me up on the beach like a banana." That thought doesn't occur to David.

So we were literally the only people on the beach from maybe where we were to Miami, and our son is in the water. Gae looks at me with that "you're the dad, do something" look, and all I can think is, *What happened to the normal teenage kid who likes to lie on the couch in a warm apartment and listen to Itunes and text his friends all day and watch old shows and eat?*

GOD

Sometimes I think when God created the oceans, he was thinking of David. He thought for a kid who struggles to get his body to do some of the things other kids can do, to go in the direction he would hope it would go in, I want to create a place where this child feels most alive, most free, where he can feel and touch and taste the *wildness of God,* even if he isn't sure how to say it or even what it is. He just knows that when he is in that ocean he is free. He is no longer a "kid with disabilities," a kid who struggles to run or to walk. He is alive, weightless, floating, feeling, laughing, and the blood is pumping rapidly through his veins . . . being held in the precious hand of God.

STORY OF LEGION

Mark 5:1 says, "They went across the lake to the region of the Gerasenes." This was a *bad neighborhood* and the disciples knew it. *Good people,* certainly good Jews, didn't go through here unless they had to. And they didn't have to. But Jesus said, "Get in the boat, we are going over to the other side." So they did.

I remember when Gae and I were first married. We moved into a small apartment on New Jersey Avenue in Washington, DC just across from Dunbar High School.

There was a large housing project just down the street that was built in the late '60s by the Catholic Church named Sursum Corda. This was the mid '80s—the crack epidemic had just hit DC, and we were quickly becoming the murder capital of the world. Marion Barry, our mayor, was in full force, and there I was with my beautiful, blonde-haired-blued-eyed-Texas-native wife, married all of about two weeks, walking together through one of the toughest, most difficult, hardened, and drug-infested communities in DC.

Gae looked at me at one point and said, "I think this is where we should start. This is where God would have us."

I thought, *You have to be crazy! We will get annihilated down here. We won't last five days.* We were there seven years. We had crossed over to "the region of the Gerasenes."

POSSESSED

No sooner had Jesus landed on shore before this man who is described as being a "man with an evil spirit," a man so strong and so possessed he breaks the chains and the shackles on his feet and cuts himself, a man no one can subdue, a man unclothed and out of his mind, runs to Jesus.

At that point, I would be saying, "Everybody back in the boat! Hurry!" Not Jesus. I wonder how many times over the course of three years these guys thought, "I can't believe we are doing this. This is nuts."

The man shouts, "What do you want with me, Jesus, Son of the Most High God?" The demons knew him. And they feared him. They knew their power was no match for the power of the Most High God.

COME OUT

"Come out of him you evil spirit." They begged him and he "gave them permission," and the evil spirits came out and went into the pigs (*v. 13*). Power. The Bible says that they "rushed down the hill and into the lake and were drowned." They were about two thousand in number. Two thousand! That is a lot of pigs. Can you imagine that farmer standing there looking at this and thinking, "Someone is going to pay for this."

At that point, the disciples look at each other and say, "Okay, this is crazy. I've never seen anything like that." People who think that following Jesus might be boring are not following this Jesus.

FULLY ALIVE

The people of the town catch wind of it and they come running out to the tombs. There they see the man, who only moments ago was thrashing about naked and breaking chains, "clothed, in his right mind, and sitting at the feet of Jesus." He was fully restored—mind, body, and spirit.

There is something right, something holy, something profound, something strong yet vulnerable, something even deeply spiritual about being fully alive, about touching the *wildness of God*. David feels that when he is in the ocean, when he feels the pounding of the waves, the surge of the water. I feel that when I am with him. Others, I think, feel that when they watch him. This man, after the powerful touch of Jesus, was now, maybe for the first time, fully and completely alive.

BACK IN THE BOAT

You might think Jesus hangs around and spends some time with this guy or goes into town and preaches a couple of great sermons. Nope. The very next line says, "As Jesus was getting back in the boat." He had risked the lives of his disciples, rowed all the way across the lake, went to this crazy, foreign land for this one man.

"So the man went away and began to tell in the Decapolis how much Jesus had done for him. And all the people were amazed."

Maybe Jesus was preaching a sermon.

JOURNAL

In what place or circumstance, much like David does in the water, do you feel most alive? What makes you feel that way?

_____

_____

_____

_____

_____

How do you see and experience the power and courage of Jesus in this passage? What surprises you, encourages you, and challenges you about this encounter with Legion?

_____

_____

_____

_____

_____

What is it about following God that feels like a _crazy adventure_ to you? What is he asking you to do? Are you willing to "get in the boat" and start rowing to the other side of the lake?

_____

_____

_____

_____

_____

PRAY

Jesus, thank you for vast oceans and boogie boards and big waves and places where I feel completely alive. Thank you for places like "across the lake," tough places, foreign places, where you sometimes call us to go. I ask you to lead me, no matter where it takes me, and give me the courage to follow. I am in the boat.

2

Beloved

"You are my Son, whom I love" (Luke 3:22).

READ

Psalm 36
Luke 3:21-23
John 1:10-13

SILENCE.

When David was born, Gae and I, like most parents, kicked around a ton of names: Nicholas, Cody, Dirk (she's from Texas), Alamo (just kidding), Nate, Josh, Justin, Thomas, Daniel, James, and then we hit on David.

David means *beloved, cherished,* and we thought, no matter what, no matter what anyone ever says or how he's treated or what someone says to him, no matter what the world sees or values or doesn't value, no matter what happens from here on out, whenever this boy hears his name, we want him to think one thing—"I am loved."

LITTLE BOY

I think of how life started for me. From the time I was a little boy, I learned that achievement felt good. I learned to win. I learned to be first. I hated being last. I learned to get things done. I learned to perform. I learned to lead. And all of that felt real good.

As I got older, I somehow began to confuse *achievement* with being loved. To me, if I did well on a test or had a great game or was elected class president or made a good speech or said something funny and people laughed or if I just knew that people liked me and wanted me on their team, for whatever the reason, it felt good and I was loved, or so I thought.

When I came to know Jesus, or what I knew of Jesus, I quickly translated this same paradigm into my relationship with God. I made God work. Love was something you earned. You earned approval—whether it was from teachers or coaches or parents or peers or God. Love wasn't free.

EARN IT

I am now fifty-six and have *worked* for God for most of my life, well over thirty years. And I still, to this day, struggle with the idea that God just loves me. He just does. He really doesn't need me or even really want me to do anything—really, anything—to earn it. In fact, he tells me I can't earn it.

I think sometimes of the prodigal son coming home and how he protested the idea of being the Father's son. He said, "I am not worthy to be called your son, make me one of your hired men." Why? Because if I am one of your hired men, I can earn it, I can go out and work for what I get, I can feel good about it, and what's maybe even better—I don't owe anybody anything because everything I got, I worked for. Wow.

THIS IS MY SON

In *Luke 3* John baptizes Jesus and the Holy Spirit descends on him like a dove and a voice from heaven says, "This is my son whom I love and in whom I am well pleased." Really? What had Jesus done up to that point that God was so pleased about? We're only in *Luke 3*.

He hasn't raised Lazarus from the dead or calmed the sea or walked on water or healed the blind man. He hasn't changed water to wine or said great things like "I am the resurrection and the life" or "I am the way, the truth, and the life." He hasn't defended a poor woman caught in adultery or healed a woman with a blood issue. He hasn't preached on the mountainside to five thousand or told Peter to cast his nets on the right side of the boat. He certainly hasn't gone to the cross or been resurrected or done any of those heroics.

And he was loved? He was God's beloved?

When God looked at him he smiled. He was "well pleased."

He delighted in him. This is *my boy*. And I love him. I just do. It has nothing to do with what he has done or will do. God just flat out loved him for being him—and Jesus knew it. He loved being loved.

DAVID

David maybe can't read above a first-grade level. He can add, sort of, but really can't subtract too well. He has never made a speech, never batted clean up, never started for his varsity football team, never run for class president, and knows almost nothing about church history or U.S. history or even that there is such a thing as history. He is not a senior vice president, he doesn't work sixty hours a week, and he has never bought a house or lived in the right neighborhood or sent his kids to private school. But this one thing he does know, beyond any shadow of a doubt—that boy knows he's loved, and he just flat out wallows in it.

He'll never make a lot of money. He'll never have a "big" job. By any measure in our society and culture, he won't be *successful*. But you can't get that boy off the dance floor. He's not self-conscious. He doesn't so much think or care about who's looking at him. He doesn't need your approval at all.

He is fully aware, fully in tune, and completely swallowed up by the fact, the absolute fact, that he is loved. And he knows it. And it just flows out of him. Out of every pore of his being.

FREE GIFT

In *Ephesians*, Paul says that this faith, this life in Jesus, this thing we cling to, our salvation, what we talk about and work so hard for, this amazing journey of grace, is a "free gift of God that no one should boast." A free gift. Something so precious, so amazing, so costly, so utterly powerful, and so life changing and life giving that you can't earn it. You can't. Even if you wanted to you can't. You can only accept it and embrace it.

How much difference does that make? How much more sure, more confident, more self-assured would you be? How less frantic and panicked are you when you stand on the solid ground that you are simply loved—just as you are? How many more risks can you take, how many silly things can you do, how much more whole and healed and powerful are you when you know, you really know, you deeply know, that the Lord of the Universe, the God that made all we can see or even imagine, the God by whom all things were created and in whom all things hold together, that God, that God loves you and loves you crazy—just for who you are?

You are indeed *the boss of the dance floor*. Now get out there and show them what you got.

JOURNAL

How do you experience *being loved*? Are you one who needs to *earn it*? What would it feel like to be loved just as you are, just because you are?

_____

_____

_____

_____

_____

How did Jesus experience love? How did he feel and understand the love of the Father?

_____

_____

_____

_____

_____

What does it mean for you to be his *beloved*; the one he runs to, the one he died for, the one he loves no matter what? What does it mean for you to be his son or daughter, to know that nothing you do can make him love you any more or any less?

_____

_____

_____

_____

_____

PRAY

Jesus, I admit today that you love me, that I am yours, that you would move mountains for me, that you literally "satisfy my desires with good things." I am your son or daughter. I am your beloved. I confess that I often act like one of your "hired men." Today, I trust your love for me. I simply receive it. You are so good, so gracious, and your love is perfect.

3

Authenticity

*"As Jesus started on his way, a man ran up to him
and fell on his knees before him" (Mark 10:17).*

READ

Psalm 77
Mark 10:17-22

SILENCE.

I sometimes think about how much time and energy I spend managing my image. I have a fairly clear idea of what I want people to think when they think of me: deep; spiritual; hard worker; producer; achiever; good communicator; funny; fun to be with; sensitive; mentor; leader; servant; pastor; friend; someone who has time and wants to spend it with them; someone people naturally want to be with; someone others will seek out; someone who gets things done; someone you need if you have a big project to do; if you need someone to really go after something you think of me; popular; energetic; high-level; charismatic; visionary; trustworthy; humble; recognized; respected; on it; punctual; doesn't rest; superhuman.

Just thinking about all that stuff makes me tired. It's exhausting to be me. You have no idea. I have a lot happening over here. I have a lot to manage.

RICH, YOUNG, POWERFUL

This guy comes to Jesus, who the Bible describes as being a *ruler* of *great wealth*. Other accounts also refer to him as *young*. So he is young, powerful, and wealthy. Wow. He has the full package: nice car; nice suit; sharp dresser; in tiptop shape; nice hair; perfect; beautiful wife; absolutely perfect kids—smart, outgoing, athletic, polite; beautiful home; perfect neighborhood; neighbors are sharp; perfect lawn, never dry or patchy; great golfer; loves the outdoors; tan; athletic; likes the beach in the summer; runs on the beach; coffee is hot; golden retriever; water is warm; towels are fluffy. Perfect. Nothing is ever dirty or out of place. It is all just *perfect.*

"Got one question," he says to Jesus. "Pretty much have it nailed, just wondering on this one thing—maybe a little more than I can fully control or expect to be in charge of. Just thinking, Jesus, since I have you here, what must I do to inherit eternal life?. . . I mean, life, I got life. I'm on that, obviously. I'm just kinda thinking of the *eternal* part, like *life after life* would seem to be more in your job description, being a rabbi and religious and stuff."

LOVED HIM

I don't think in a purely natural sense that this would have been Jesus' guy; Jesus was more attracted to the hardworking, blue-collar, fisherman type—guys with nets, out all night, sweaty, working hard, muddy, cigarettes, camo hats, boots, maybe a tat or two. But almost the next line says, "Jesus looked at him and loved him." He felt compassion for him. Much like he looked at the leper in *Mark 1* and "had compassion on him," he looked at this young man and honestly loved him.

He first says, "You know the commandments: Do not murder, do not commit adultery, do not steal, do not give false testimony, do not defraud, honor your father and mother" (*Mark 10:19*).

ELATED

The man is elated. "I got this! I told you! I am rich. I am young. I am powerful. And . . . I am a good boy!

"I've done all these things since I was a boy," he declared.

I couldn't say that. Not sure I could give you a nod on any of them. This guy could. And I don't think he was faking it. Jesus didn't say he was faking it. I think he agreed. You got 'em.

"What a great answer, Jesus. Thank you," said the man. "Hey, I'll catch you. I got to go." He turns.

GO AND SELL

"You know, Jim, just one more thing," Jesus says. The man pauses. "Go and sell all you have, and give it to the poor. And then come follow me."

Honestly, I don't think this is a trick question. I don't think Jesus is trying to embarrass him or show him up or teach him a lesson. I don't think he is trying to teach his disciples something or the crowd or anybody. I think he genuinely loves this guy and wants him to follow him. He wants his heart above all else, not his money or his possessions. Jesus knows that this one thing stands between the two of them and he is willing to ask him for it. Money, possessions, stuff, and image has a grip on this guy, and he has a pretty firm grip on them.

Money and the stuff that comes with it is his identity. It is who he is. To lose it would be to lose everything about him. It would be tantamount to what the disciples did in *Luke 5* where it says, "They left everything and followed Jesus." He is not ready for that. He's just not.

FACE FELL

"At this the man's face fell." Crushed. Done. Disappointed. Hurt. Broken. Sad. He walked home. There was a lot to manage.

Jesus was sad.

FULL ON FREEDOM

David has very little to manage. When he is happy, sad, frustrated, hungry, tired, or sleepy you know it—he is literally the most authentic person I know. No filters. He couldn't hide it if he wanted to.

I sometimes wonder how different the world would be if Christians, followers of Jesus, would simply be honest with each other. Honest. "Hey, I'm hurting over here. I got nothing. I am afraid. I am angry. My kids are struggling. I need help. My wife is sick. I messed up. Pretty bad."

What keeps us from that? What are we so afraid of? We are killing ourselves. We hide. We medicate. We control. We manage. We do everything we can to keep the lid on. We don't sleep at night. We share the easiest, cleanest, most acceptable bit possible and then lock the rest in a trunk and try to hide it.

I look at David and think, *Why can't I live like that?* He has no trunk.

Jesus was the most authentic, honest, truthful, humble, loving person that ever walked the face of the earth. He certainly could have stopped with this man after the first lap and said, "Hey, sounds like you're good, you've done a lot, thank you. Eternal life. Should be good." No! He's not good. And Jesus has the guts to tell him.

HONEST

I am getting older. And one thing I keep telling myself is, "I want to be more honest." Stop hiding. Cut the bullshit. Really. Life is hard. Hard crap happens all the time. If this thing is not about being honest and leading deep, authentic, truthful lives then Jesus died for absolutely nothing—it's all a joke.

We are forgiven! We are free! We are sinners *saved by grace!* Get over it. You are not perfect. That's the whole point. Twelve steps. Admit that you just don't have it all together—oh, and you never will. You're only hope, my only hope, our absolute only hope in this life and the one to come, is Jesus, is the cross of Christ, the blood he shed on yours and my behalf. He died so we can be honest. Who are you kidding for crying out loud! Give up!

Ephesians 4:25 in the *Message Bible* says, "What this adds up to, then, is this: no more lies, no more pretense. Tell your neighbor the truth. In Christ's body we're all connected to each other, after all. When you lie to others, you end up lying to yourself."

I don't want to lie. I want to live honest and free. No more pretenses. No more management. I want to be like David. And like Jesus, deep, authentic, truthful.

JOURNAL

What is it that you are afraid to tell someone or talk about? What does it mean for you to manage an *image*? What parts of you do you feel like you are *managing*?

_____

_____

_____

_____

_____

What would it mean for you to live an authentic life? How did Jesus live authentically? If he were to ask you to give up this one thing, "go and sell it," "leave it," what would it be?

_____

_____

_____

_____

_____

How does what Jesus did on the cross set you free and allow you to be honest? How might your life change if you really believed that?

_____

_____

_____

_____

_____

PRAY

Jesus, we start today by simply acknowledging what you did for us on the cross. We are forgiven sinners. We aren't perfect. In fact, we are far from it. You know it, and we know it. And today, we want to be honest—there are places where we are hurting, places where we are hiding, things we are holding onto—you died for those places and those things as well, Jesus. You want us to bring them into the light. You want us to be free and to be whole.

4

Advocate

*"But when he, the Spirit of truth, comes,
he will guide you into all truth" (John 16:13).*

READ

Psalm 121
John 16:5-16
Acts 2:1-4

SILENCE.

I love the idea of having an advocate—someone who loves you enough to stand up for you, someone who steps in, someone who represents you, someone maybe older, wiser, and stronger, and someone who says, "I not only know him, but I love him, and I am willing to fight for him. I will protect him. I am there for him."

I always loved my grandfather Pop-pop. Both he and Mimi were very young when I was a kid. He was a DC firefighter for over twenty years and then retired on disability when he was fifty. Fifty!

So he and Mimi were always at all my games. They picked me up sometimes after practice or took me to school. My brother, sister, and I would stay at their house when my parents were out of town. We would watch games, go fishing, and play catch together. He was much more than a granddad. He was more like my best friend.

Any time I had an issue or needed something, I knew I could go to Pop-pop. He believed in me. He trusted me. He always wanted the best for me.

In an even greater, and maybe in a more tangible and consistent way, Gae and I are always doing the same for David.

THE WORLD

What you realize pretty quickly is that the world is not set up for people like David. People don't mean to but he is just left out. Schools don't know how to include him. Buses, subways, restaurants, airplanes, grocery stores, doctor offices—there are very few places you can go with David where you don't feel like saying, "I'm going to need some help here." Other kids, even other families, just don't know how to include him—so they don't.

Unfortunately, maybe one of the hardest places is at church. He just doesn't fit.

And so you learn—almost on every occasion—to ask for help.

People often wonder why parents of kids with disabilities seem so *ticked off* all the time. It is because they are either gearing up for or coming down from a fight. They are exhausted. Every situation they walk into they have to first think, *How is my son or daughter going to react to this? Is it too noisy, too crowded, too loud, too hard to understand, overwhelming, hot, cold, you name it. Where are the exits? What will we do if we have to leave?*

FINDING A GOOD SCHOOL

Easily the most difficult thing we did when we moved to New York was trying to find a school for David. We applied to a private school for kids with disabilities. It would have been perfect. Less than a month before we moved, we were turned down.

We went to work on other private schools and couldn't find one that looked suitable for David that wasn't already full. So we turned to the public schools. We were moving at the end of July. No one would call us back. When we finally did get a hold of someone, they encouraged us to call back at the end of August. August? Don't they start school in August?

Finally, after what seemed like hundreds of calls and multiple meetings, he was finally placed—PS 54, Booker T. Washington on 107th St. on the Upper West Side.

We thought we had done our job. In reality, it was just starting.

BUS SERVICE

He didn't have bus service. So we had to figure out a way to get him to the school and pick him up. We had sold our car. So it was taxi or the subway. He also didn't have a one-on-one paraprofessional or teacher's aide. So we had to apply for one.

We didn't have another option, so when the first day came, we stood out on Central Park West with David in his school clothes and backpack and hailed a cab. That cab was our school bus. Twelve dollars and a lecture from the cabbie later, we jumped out of the cab and headed for the school.

AN HOUR LATER

Only one problem, David wasn't with us. He had plopped down as soon as he hit the sidewalk and was sitting there with backpack on, legs crossed, looking at the ground, refusing to move. It wasn't that David wouldn't go in the school. He wouldn't even get close to it. We were still a good fifty yards from the entrance. And so, the battle was on.

We encouraged, prodded, gave him incentives—even threatened. An hour later, an hour of sitting on the sidewalk with people walking around him and over him, we had him within ten feet of the door. Finally, we got him in. We declared victory and headed for home. Less than thirty minutes later the school called and asked us to come pick him up. Apparently David never made it into the classroom.

MONTHS

This went on for a couple of months. We would get him in the door, they would meet him, and two hours later they would call us to come pick him up. He was scared to death. Gae got to the point where she didn't even go home. She just walked across the street to the coffee shop and waited for the school to call.

We met with the principal. We met with the teacher. We met with the head of Special Ed at the school. We spoke with parents. We eventually got him a one-on-one. He was still scared. Finally, we had to say this isn't working. We took David out of school and brought him home. The search was on for the next school.

THE ADVOCATE

Here's what the Bible says: "But I tell you the truth: It is for your good that I am going away. Unless I go away, the Counselor (or Advocate) will not come to you, but when I go, I will send him to you. . . . But when he, the Spirit of truth comes, he will guide you into all truth. He will not speak on his own, he will speak only what he hears, and he will tell you what is yet to come" (*John 16:7,13*).

Later he tells the disciples: "But you will receive power when the Holy Spirit comes upon you; and you will be my witnesses" (*Acts 1:8*).

Wow. How great is that. One of the first things Jesus does when he sees the disciples after the resurrection is he "breathes on them the Holy Spirit" (*John 20:22*). So we have this one in us who loves us, who speaks words to us, who gives us knowledge and wisdom, who speaks the words of Jesus to us, who goes before us, who *advocates* for us, who gives us power, real power—to heal, to trust, to have faith, to believe, to be patient, and to be kind and joyful and loving. Who in every situation is thinking, "What are they going to need here?"

AFRICA

Perhaps one of the greatest deficits we have here in what I would call *the West* is we don't really understand or believe the Holy Spirit. We, in a sense, deny its power.

Our son Michael was in Africa, Tanzania, with Young Life last summer. When we go to camp here in the U.S., we go to camp. We pick up our staff and our leaders, we pack our bags, we get the kids, and we go to camp. When they go to camp in Africa, they bring a team of exorcists with them. I'm not kidding.

This group has one job and one job only—to cast demons out of kids. Really? Have we ever done that here in the U.S.? Why not? Mostly because we simply don't understand it or even believe it. We don't get that maybe what is going on inside a lot of kids is more of a spiritual battle than a physical one. We also don't fully understand the power, the real power that is available to us through the Holy Spirit. We have never seen it, and we don't believe it.

POWER

I want to live a powerful life—full of passion and courage and strength. I want to believe God for big, crazy things.

I think often of David and how as we were going through that battle with finding the right school, it was just not enough to show up every so often. As his parents, his *advocates*, we showed up every day. And we would do everything we could to fight for him.

But when you think of the Holy Spirit, the real Advocate, that is a completely different story. When the Spirit shows up things move, things change.

In *Acts 2* the Spirit came like a "violent, rushing wind" and with what "seemed to be tongues of fire." That is real power. Then Peter stood up, filled with that same Spirit, and three thousand people came to Christ; or how in *Acts 3* he looked at a poor beggar and said, "Silver and gold I do not have, but what I have I give to you. In the name of Jesus of Nazareth, walk"—that kind of power. It is the same God, the same Holy Spirit, and he lives in us, and he is pressing into this place, this world of darkness with his unbelievable power and light. "Thy kingdom come, thy will be done . . ."

JOURNAL

Who plays the role of *advocate* in your life? How do you play that role for others?

_____

_____

_____

_____

_____

What is it you believe about the Holy Spirit? How is he your *advocate*? Where is it that you deny his power?

_____

_____

_____

_____

_____

What does it mean for you to live a powerful life? How do you invite the Spirit in? If you did, what difference would that make in your life and the lives of those around you?

_____

_____

_____

_____

_____

PRAY

Today, Jesus, I thank you for the gift of the Holy Spirit. Thank you that in him I have an Advocate—a protector, a counselor, a leader, and a provider—someone who goes on my behalf. Let me wait, let me wait and listen. Come, Holy Spirit, fill me today. I want to live a powerful life, filled with the power of the Holy Spirit. I believe you, Jesus. Speak to me, dear Jesus—give me your wisdom, your strength, your courage, and your life.

5

Shrink Me

"And you are to give him the name Jesus" (Luke 1:31).

READ

Psalm 25
Luke 1:26-38

SILENCE.

David's world is often quite different from my world or your world. David's world is only limited by one's imagination. In his world, if you can imagine it, you can do it.

Last summer we were walking around the Great Lawn in Central Park. At one point David gets down, actually lays down on his belly, and is looking through the fence. You can see the wheels turning.

I get down and lay on my belly so I can see what David is seeing. Our noses are pressed up against the wire of the fence and we are staring into the deep, green grass. There are literally hundreds of people looking at us, stepping around us, wondering what we are looking at. Real people, leading real lives.

Finally he looks at me and says, "Shrink me, Daddy."

I said, "What? 'Shrink me.' Shrink you? How am I going to do that?"

"I want to go in there."

"You want to go in there? Yea. Well, I don't think I can help you much, son. See, David, that's a movie, it's called a *story*; it's what we refer to as *make believe*.

"As adults, as real people in this world, we have a pretty hard line between what we understand to be the real world and the world of what we call *fantasy* or *make believe*. Right now, you are living in the world of fantasy."

None of that seemed to make a dent in David. He was only more determined.

"Shrink me!" he stammered. "I want to go in there."

I was at a loss. So in my grown up voice I said, "And then what are you going to do? Go battle the giant ants and potato bugs of the Great Lawn?"

ANGELS

"In the sixth month," the Bible says, "God sent the angel Gabriel to Nazareth, a town in Galilee, to a virgin pledged to be married to a man named Joseph, a descendent of David." Really? Are we supposed to believe that? An angel? With wings and stuff? And his name was Gabriel? Do they all have names? And where was he before he appeared to this virgin who was pledged to be married? Hanging out in heaven? And God sent him? Can you imagine God saying, "Hey, Gabriel, can you come here a second? I have a little something for you."

What world is this?

So the angel goes to Mary and says, "Greetings you who are highly favored. The Lord is with you." Okay. This is really starting to get crazy. An angel appears to this random virgin and begins telling her she is highly favored and that the Lord is with her.

Mary is puzzled.

It gets better. "You will be with child and give birth to a son, and you are to give him the name Jesus. He will be great and be called the Son of the Most High. The Lord God will give him the throne of his father David, and he will reign over the house of Jacob forever; his kingdom will never end."

"How will this be," Mary asked the angel, "since I am a virgin?"

SON OF THE MOST HIGH

Have we just read this story a few too many times? Do we have any idea, any crazy, unearthly idea, what is going on here? Are we just too numb, too grown up, too one dimensional, seen one too many Christmas pageants?

This is insane. The literal God of the universe has just announced to a virgin named Mary by way of an angel named Gabriel that she is going to have a baby and this baby will be "the

Son of the Most High!" God!

And if that is not enough, in the next verse he goes on to say, "The Holy Spirit will come upon you." To which I say, "Stop it right there." So she is going to get pregnant, but not from being with any man. She is going to get pregnant from the Holy Spirit? She's having God's baby? Anything else you can think of here, Gabriel? This has been a pretty interesting visit so far.

"The power of the Most High will overshadow you. So the holy one to be born will be called the Son of God." This is no ordinary baby. This isn't just someone who scores well on the SAT or goes to Princeton on a scholarship. This is going to be the Son of God for crying out loud!

How do we come to be so immune to such unbelievable craziness? The God of the Universe is bursting into history in the form of a baby, born to this young, little, innocent virgin named Mary who was visited and spoken to by an angel, who became pregnant by the Holy Spirit, and most of us turn the page and think, *Wow, isn't that nice.* Really?

And what does she say. "No way! I don't believe you! Get out of my house! This is nuts!"

No, instead the Bible says, "'I am the Lord's servant,' Mary answered, 'May it be to me as you have said.'"

Then the angel left her. And just before he left, he looked back at Mary and said, "Nothing is impossible with God."

ALL THINGS ARE POSSIBLE

For David, all things are possible. When he says, "Shrink me," he's really not kidding. He is not limited by what we conventionally think we should be able to do.

I want to trust God that way—this God who showed up at Mary's doorstep, who walked on water, who calmed the sea, who raised Lazarus and healed Bartimaeus, who changed water into wine and fed five thousand on a hillside, the God who "created all things and in whom all things hold together," the one who said, "I am the resurrection and the life. He who believes in me will live."

I want to worship that God, I want to know that God, I want to wait on and listen to and trust in that God—I want my

God to be that big, that strong, that powerful, that mighty, that unpredictable.

I want to know a different reality, beyond what we can see or feel. I want a God-sized reality, a God-informed, David-like reality. If God can imagine it, it can happen reality. I want to be child-like enough that I can believe it.

I want to look up at the stars and wonder. I want to look out at the ocean and dream. I want to lie down on my bed at night and think that was unbelievable. I want to live each day with Gabriel looking back at me saying, "All things, all things, all things are possible with God."

JOURNAL

What areas or places in your life do you have a hard time believing God will show up?

_____

_____

_____

_____

_____

Think of a time when you felt like God asked you to believe him for something crazy, something impossible?

_____

_____

_____

_____

_____

How would life be different if you actually believed God for those things? That not only could he show up, he could change things, he could make things new, he could bring light and life to really hard places?

_____

_____

_____

_____

_____

PRAY

Thank you, Jesus, that all things are possible in you, that you are the Holy One, the Almighty, the Living God—even "the wind and the waves obey you." Let me trust you and believe you today for big things, for the places in my life and work that are hard for me to trust. I believe you, Jesus.

6

Suffering

*"When the Lord saw her, his heart went out to her
and he said, 'Don't cry'" (Luke 7:13).*

READ

Psalm 23
Luke 7:11-17
Mark 5:21-43

SILENCE.

Some years ago, a couple gave birth to a son. As with any birth, this couple was ecstatic at the sight of their newborn baby. Although there had been some indication in earlier sonograms that there may be difficulties with this child, everything seemed to be normal. It was their third child, and after one miscarriage this couple could not have been happier.

And then, something went deadly wrong. The nurse noticed that the child's eyes were a little farther apart than normal, that his ears were smaller and lower, that his face was somewhat flat, that the crease on his hand ran directly across the palm, that his legs were shorter, his fingers stubbier, his neck thicker, his muscle tone floppier. The baby's mother held the child and knew that something wasn't right, that something was different.

Upstairs a pager rang and a neonatologist was summoned to the birthing room to examine the baby. As the doctor measured the newborn, the couple clutched each others hands studying the doctor's face for any signs of hope or good news.

DOWN SYNDROME

The doctor turned, and for the first time, the couple heard the words, Down syndrome.

Instantly their world came crashing down around them.

Their birth had become a death. What had been a crowning moment had become a crushing defeat not for today or for tomorrow, but for the rest of their lives.

Other doctors, specialists, and social workers were brought in to brief the couple. Heart defects, vision problems, hearing loss, epileptic seizures, and Alzheimer's were discussed freely in tandem with mental retardation, speech problems, and lack of coordination and motor ability. The reality of loneliness, special classes, therapies, living arrangements, and trust funds came over the couple like a dark cloud.

Obviously this was a mistake. Obviously these people had made a mistake. Obviously God had made a mistake. Obviously someone did not know what they were doing. Finally they all left, and the couple was alone with their child for the first time. Alone in their anger and tears, alone asking the question, "Why us, why now, why this?"

NAIN

To be a parent is to know suffering. It just comes with the territory. There really is no way around it.

There are two powerful stories of parents in the Gospels. We encounter the first in *Luke 7*. It starts, "Soon afterward, Jesus went to a town called Nain." Nain is a tiny mountain town in Galilee. The Gospel doesn't tell us why Jesus went there—only that he did and that, as in most cases, "a crowd followed him."

As he came into town a procession was leaving. It was a procession of suffering and pain. A boy had died, the "only son of his mother," a mother who was also a widow. She had buried her husband and now she was burying her only son. Her life had been filled with deep hurt, anguish, and misery.

She also knew that without a husband or a son, the prospects of her making a living were slim. She was now left to a life of loneliness, isolation, hardship, and poverty.

PROCESSION OF LIFE

This is the procession that Jesus encounters. And as he does, a procession of life meets a procession of death. The Bible says that when Jesus saw the woman "his heart went out to her." I think of how many people I see in the city that your heart just breaks for them. So Jesus stops and looks at her and says, "Don't cry." Almost to reassure her, to say, "It is okay. It is going to be okay. I'm here now."

He touches the coffin and says, "Young man, I say to you, get up." And the boy sits up. And now with both crowds looking on in awe, the Bible says, "Jesus gave him back to his mother." Can you feel the power of that moment—this heartbroken mom, a crowd of onlookers, a boy raised and now given back—hope, awe, praise, wonder, power, tears, gladness, joy, and the deep healing of a broken heart. Now two processions become one big celebration.

A SYNAGOGUE RULER

The other story is in *Mark 5*, where Jesus had just crossed over the lake and once again a large crowd gathered around him. And this man, a synagogue ruler named Jairus, came there. Seeing Jesus, he fell at his feet and pleaded earnestly with him, "My daughter is dying. Please put your hand on her so that she will be healed and live."

I love the next line. "So Jesus went with him." He didn't just say, "Go home, she'll be fine." Or maybe what I would have said, "Don't you see I have a huge crowd here? I can't leave now." No, he felt and saw the pain of this father, and not only did he want to heal his daughter, he wanted to be with this man and take the time to walk with him home.

And then, as we know, something very odd happens. A woman in the crowd touches him and he feels power go out of him. She is healed immediately. And Jesus begins to look around and ask, "Who touched me?"

Finally, the woman knowing what had happened "came and fell at his feet trembling." And the Bible says Jesus "listened to her whole story." Now if you are Jairus at this point, who is a pretty big deal in this town, whose daughter is dying, you might be thinking, "Are you kidding me? She's fine. Let's go here, fella."

DON'T BE AFRAID

To make matters worse, while all this is going on, a group of men come from the house of Jairus to tell him, "Why bother the teacher any more. Your daughter is dead." There couldn't be any more painful words in the English language.

"Don't be afraid, just believe," Jesus said. Those are five words that should pretty much sum up our life in Christ.

When they came to Jairus's house there was a commotion. The reality of what the men had said on the road now comes over Jairus like a penetrating, choking fog. People are "crying and wailing loudly." Jairus's twelve-year-old daughter lies motionless on the bed. As he gets close to the house, he sinks into his own deep anguish, wailing, and pain. No reason to hustle now.

Again, Jesus enters in. "The child is not dead, but asleep," Jesus says. He asks everyone to leave the house and brings with him the parents as well as Peter, James, and John.

And then going over to the little girl, lying there motionless, he says almost the exact words that he said to the little boy in Nain, "Little girl, I say to you, get up."

And she does.

And the Bible says, "She begins to walk around the house." I love that. Little show off. People are stunned and amazed.

Then, as he often does, Jesus tells them not to tell anyone. Can you imagine? "Oh, Jesus just raised this little girl from the dead. I think I'll go home and not tell anyone." He'd better be glad my grandmother wasn't there.

"Get her something to eat," Jesus says, and those in the crowd started making peanut butter and jelly sandwiches.

RAISING A CHILD

Someone once told me raising a child with a disability is a permanent grief. I would say that is true. There are days when I think of those first days in the hospital or times even now when I see David struggle or some kid stare at him on the playground or I think too far into the future, and I can tear up pretty quickly.

But here is the deeper reality, a deeper truth, not just for a parent with a kid with a disability but also for anyone who has known suffering and known it deeply: "Those who have passed over (through their suffering) eventually find a much bigger world of endurance, meaning, hope, self-esteem, deeper and true desire, but most especially, a bottomless pool of love both within and without. Their treasure hunt is over, and they are home, home free!" (Rohr, *Breathing Underwater, p. 124*).

Unbeknownst to us, seventeen years ago that was the gift God was giving us, the opportunity to come home, to find a bigger world of "endurance, meaning, hope, and a bottomless pool of love" wrapped in a little bundle of joy we named David.

JOURNAL

How have you been wounded or suffered as a person? Where was Jesus in the midst of that suffering? How did that time change you?

_____

_____

_____

_____

_____

How does Jesus enter into the suffering of the widow of Nain and of Jairus? Apart from restoring their kids to life, how does he show that he cares?

_____

_____

_____

_____

_____

I've heard it said, "Suffering strips everything else away and allows us to see that which is most important." How has God done that in your life? How has walking through suffering allowed you to "come home"?

_____

_____

_____

_____

_____

PRAY

Dear Jesus, thank you that you are not distant, that your compassion and love allows you to move toward us. We are not alone. You are with us, you hear us, you sit close to us, you listen to us, and you are with us in our loneliness and grief. You suffered unspeakable hurt and pain on the cross on our behalf. Hold us now. Let us wait with you. Restore us. Bring us home. You are good. You are strong. You are able. And you are here.

7

Alone

"Here a great number of disabled people used to lie" (John 5:4).

READ

Psalm 88
John 5:1-14

SILENCE.

David spends a good part of his days alone. If he is not at school or another extracurricular activity that we have enrolled him in—swimming, basketball, drama, art—then he is home alone, with us.

Upon this writing, David is seventeen. He has never been invited over to a friend's house to play or had a friend over. He has never been invited to a birthday party or to the park. He has never just gone outside and played with a group of friends. He has never been chosen to play on a baseball team or basketball team. His closest friends are by far his sister and brother, his mom, and me.

Disability in our culture is often synonymous with loneliness and isolation. It is the pain of not being seen or noticed, of being *invisible*.

One of the great tragedies of our fast-paced, lightning-speed, texting, Snapchat, Facebook culture is that we simply lose those who can't keep up. They are almost predestined to be alone, marginalized, unseen, and unnoticed because they aren't fast enough, quick enough, smart enough, social enough, or verbal enough to keep up. They are slow and hard to understand. They are alone.

"You have taken my companions and loved ones from me," says the psalmist. "Darkness is my closest friend" (*Ps 88:18*).

THE SHEEP GATE

One story in the Bible that seems to embody this feeling of being alone is in *John 5*. It starts by saying, "Now there is in Jerusalem near the Sheep Gate a pool, which in Aramaic is called Bethesda and which is surrounded by five covered colonnades. Here a great number of disabled people used to lie—the blind, the lame, the paralyzed" (*v. 2-3*).

My guess is there weren't many leaders, and I would include myself in this, who used to visit this place by the Sheep Gate. The people there were the beggars, the poor, the outcasts, the lame, the discarded, and the lonely; really the ones that no one else wanted. My guess is between the sheep coming through the gate and those lying on the ground, it smelled pretty bad there.

There are so many places like that in our culture. Places like those that house the mentally ill and the disabled, shelters for the homeless, prisons (how many Christians do you know that have ever stepped foot in a prison?), schools for the *emotionally disturbed*, hospitals that house the chronically ill, nursing homes, drug rehab facilities, and refugee camps to name a few.

Yet there Jesus was. I would bet you had to be pretty intentional about going to this place. You didn't just walk past it on the way to something else. Like most things similar to this in our culture, it was hidden, off to the side; a place that if you didn't have to go there, you may not even know it existed.

As was often the case, as when he showed up at the home of Levi or was found eating with Zacchaeus or stopped for Bartimaeus or put his arm around the leper, those who were following Jesus must have thought, "Where is he going? Why are we going here? Nobody goes here, it smells, it makes me nauseous, and it's uncomfortable. I can't wait until we get out of here."

Nick Palermo, the founder of Young Life's Capernaum Ministries, says, "We have to become comfortable with being uncomfortable." That is not always easy to do.

HEART OF GOD

But here, here is the heart of God. For this man had been lying there for thirty-eight years (thirty-eight, are you kidding me?) with no one "to help him in the pool when the water is stirred." After thirty-eight years of lying in the same place, you have become invisible. People walk by you and literally don't see you. They are blind to you. You are like a street lamp, a trashcan, a part of the curb.

Nick often tells the story of when he first became a Young Life leader. He was in the high school cafeteria doing contact work and there was a whole table of kids in wheel chairs. And he asked a couple of the other leaders, "Who are those kids?"

"Don't know."

He asked some of the other kids. They didn't know. He even asked some of the teachers. "Not sure." These kids were invisible.

COMPLACENT

After thirty-eight years you would also have become fairly comfortable with your life. *Complacent* might be a better word. I think of the few men that I've known who are homeless and have lived on the streets for an extended time. They really don't know much else. They have become fairly acclimated to their life. It's what they know. It's not good or easy, it is actually very hard, but it is what they know.

It sounds odd but then I realize there are parts of me that are sick or paralyzed or lame that have been that way for a very long time. They aren't good. In fact, there are lots of days I wish they were different. They actually smell. But they are me. They are what I have grown accustomed to. They are the parts of me, like those people lying there, which for the most part are invisible, parts that other people don't see.

DO YOU WANT TO GET WELL?

And then Jesus asks him what would seem to be a rather obvious question, "Do you want to get well?" What? *Do you want to get well?* Are you kidding me? I have been lying here for thirty-eight years. What kind of question is that?

Then I think, *What about that old, dirty blanket you are carrying around, John? It is stinky and smelly and ugly and maybe even hurts you and hurts others, but it is YOUR blanket and you've grown fairly accustomed to having it.*

Do you want to get well? Do you?

NO ONE TO HELP ME

The man has a funny answer. "Sir," the invalid replied, "I have no one to help me into the pool when the water is stirred. While I am trying to get in, someone else goes down ahead of me" (v. 7). Which again seems absurd. Here is the God of the Universe standing next to you, the one who controls the wind and the waves, the one who formed the oceans, who set the stars in the sky, and you are talking about needing someone to drag you down to the pool when the water is stirred?

And then I think about how many things I have trusted over the years to carry me other than Jesus. For some reason it is the seen things, things we can actually touch and feel, that are so easy for us to pour our trust. It is why every time Moses turned his back the Israelites were making some kind of molten calf or idol, something they could see and touch, and maybe why the first commandment is "you should have no other gods beside me," and the second is "you should not make for yourself an idol."

JESUS

But Jesus says to him, to my son David, to me, to us, "You are not alone! I see you! I notice you! You are not forgotten. You are mine, and I am yours. You are not complacent. You are not enslaved. You are free. I made you. I have given my life for you. You are whole. You are not broken. You are alive! You are fully and completely alive!"

Then Jesus said to him, "Take up your mat and walk." At once the man was cured; he picked up his mat and walked.

JOURNAL

Where do you feel most alone? When have you felt ignored or forgotten? What part of you are you hiding that no one else sees, that perhaps has been sick for a long time, that if you opened the door, it might smell a bit?

_____

_____

_____

_____

_____

Why does Jesus go to the Sheep Gate? How does he engage this man? Why does he ask him if he wants to get well? How might this man's life be different now?

_____

_____

_____

_____

_____

Does Jesus notice you? Does he see you? Does he engage you? If he asked you that same question, what would you say? What might change for you?

_____

_____

_____

_____

_____

PRAY

Dear Jesus, thank you today that you notice me, that you stop for me, that even when I find myself in lonely, stinky, hard, smelly places, when I have lost all sense of who I am and who I was created to be, when I have given up and simply become complacent—you enter in, and you bring power, freedom, courage, healing, strength, and life. I am not alone. I am yours. Thank you, Jesus.

8

Fearfully and Wonderfully Made

"So God created man in his own image, in the image of God he created him; male and female he created them" (Gen 1:27).

READ

Psalm 139
John 9:1-12

SILENCE.

The Bible starts out with such a powerful and beautiful picture of creation. It says, "In the beginning God"—not us, but God—"created the heavens and the earth." The earth, when it was first created, was "formless and void" and covered in darkness.

So God began, and he created light, and the light was good, and he separated the light from the darkness, and the "light," it says, "he called day and the darkness he called night." And then he separated the heavens from the earth and the dry land from the water. And in the water he created every creepy, crawly thing that is in the water—all kinds of sea creatures and eels and turtles and porpoise and whales and manatee and blowfish and seahorses and you name it.

And he created the mountains and the streams and jungles and dry deserts and daisies—and zebras and monkeys and hyenas and hippos and mule deer (mule deer?). And he looked at all of this and said, "It is good."

MALE AND FEMALE

Then it says he created you and me. "So God created man in his own image, in the image of God he created him, male and female he created them" (*Gen 1:27*). And then he looked at them and said, "It is very good."

Psalm 139 says, "You created my inmost being." That part of me that nobody sees or maybe even cares about, you created that part of me, the part of me where I keep some of my deepest, darkest secrets. You not only created it, you are there. You are there with me. Your image, your very likeness, is there.

It goes on to say, "You knit me together in my mother's womb." Wow.

My wife is a knitter. You know what she does? She takes real care in every stitch; every little stitch is important, and she weaves them into a pattern. And if she makes a mistake, she pulls it out and starts over. And you know what else? Each thing she makes, everything she does, is different. It is unique and it is beautiful. No one is like the other. They are masterpieces. We are indeed "fearfully and wonderfully made."

MY DAD

People have often said that I look like my dad. I also talk like my dad. I can't help it. And, what is worse, he talks like me. We sound alike, we walk alike, we think alike, we like the same food and eat the same cereal; we even wear the same pants. A couple of months ago, after a visit from my parents, this guy in our building said to me as I was getting on the elevator, "Hey, I met your dad last week."

I said, "Really? How'd you know it was my dad?"

He said, "Are you kidding? That was easy."

So when it says that we were created in God's image it means we kind of look like him, we act like him, we are creative like him, we bear his likeness, we are his masterpiece, and we are unique, unlike any other. And it also means that we are created to be in relationship with him. Just as he is, we are created to love and to be loved.

RELATIONSHIP

So now here is the God of the Universe, the one holy and true God creates us, you and me, in such a way that we are able to be in relationship with him. We see that with Adam and Eve as God places them in the garden, and then he walks around with them and he talks with them and he spends time getting to know them. It is his favorite part of his day.

And later we read in John's gospel that we know his voice much like a newborn baby instinctively knows the voice of her mother—we hear God, we sense God, he calls our name, our spirit connects with his Spirit—we live connected in relationship.

Do you know what God says when he sees all this? He says, "It is good, very good. Excellent. Perfect."

DAVID

Unfortunately, I'm not so sure that most people would say that about David. I think more often than not people would say, or probably not actually say, but maybe think, "Something went wrong there"; "God messed up"; "That's a shame"; "Wow, that must be hard."

It is hard at times, but God certainly did not mess up.

A MAN BORN BLIND

There is a great encounter in *John 9* where Jesus sees this man who had been blind from birth. And one of the disciples asked him, "Rabbi, who sinned, this man or his parents that he was born blind?" I guess it was assumed that if you were blind it was some sort of punishment for something either you had done that was really bad or your parents had done.

"Neither this man nor his parents sinned," Jesus said, "but this happened so that the work of God might be displayed in his life." Jesus seems to be saying, "This was intentional. This man, this man you see here, he was made in my image, just like you were. He was "fearfully and wonderfully made." I knit him together in his mother's womb. Stitch by stitch I carefully and masterfully knit him together, and he is my masterpiece.

"And maybe more importantly, because he is made in my image, there are parts of me that you can only see, only understand from seeing and knowing this man. I will be glorified in this man, not in spite of his differences, but because of his differences."

Paul says in his letter to the Corinthians, "But God chose the foolish things of the world to shame the wise; God chose the weak things of the world to shame the strong. God chose the lowly things of this world and the despised things—and the things that are not—to nullify the things that are" (*I Corinthians 1:27-28*).

BEAUTY

The power and the presence and the beauty and the character and the grace and glory of God leak out of David in ways he can't control. There are parts of God, of the character of God that I only can experience from knowing David. He is "fearfully and wonderfully made." He is made in God's image. There is not one part of him that is a mistake. Not a single part. He was "knit together" by the Master. He is God's masterpiece and reflects him in all his glory. He is simply and fully a gift, a God-given, beautiful gift.

Jesus spit on the ground and made some mud with the saliva. He rubbed the mud on the man's eyes and told him to go wash in the Pool of Siloam. "So the man went and washed and came home seeing."

JOURNAL

What does it mean for you to be created in the image of God? How do you experience that in your relationship with God—hear him, see him, feel him?

_____

_____

_____

_____

_____

How are you fearfully and wonderfully made? What parts of you do you not like as much? How does God see those parts? What do others say is wonderful about you that surprises you?

_____

_____

_____

_____

_____

How do you see people who are different than you—different race or ethnicity, people who are poor, people who have _special needs_ or are _disabled_? How does God see them? What can we together learn from each other?

_____

_____

_____

_____

_____

PRAY

Thank you, dear Jesus, that you created me, a perfect me, in your image, that I look like you, walk like you, talk like you—that your Spirit lives in me and above all else, you love me and desire to be in relationship with me. Thank you, Jesus, for those who look much different than me, thank you that they also reflect your glory, your diversity, and your wholeness. We are together, fearfully and wonderfully made. You knit us together. We are indeed your masterpiece.

9

Celebration and the Power of a Good Party

"For this son of mine was dead and is alive again; he was lost and is found" (Luke 15:24).

READ

Psalm 126
Luke 15:11-31

SILENCE.

David loves to celebrate. In one sense he could care less what the occasion is. Your birthday or my birthday is just as good as his birthday. Christmas could literally be any day of the year it really doesn't matter.

This past year we celebrated his birthday by having some friends over and grilling in the backyard. It was so great. David loved it. He was so excited his friends were coming over, Chase and the girls, Howard and Teak, Karen, Katie, Meghan, Gee, Ashley, a few neighbors—a great group.

It was a great party. We played games, we decorated bird houses (I know), we hid the plastic insects and went and found them, we gave out prizes, we ate cheeseburgers, and David unwrapped presents, but the penultimate, the absolute pinnacle, the place where David's face just exploded with excitement, was when we lit the candles and began singing "Happy Birthday."

There is something about that moment that is almost indescribable, something magical, something where almost every fiber, every cell, every part of his body, even his own soul, is celebrating. It is contagious. It yells, "This is awesome! . . . This is so great! . . . I am so excited I could wet my pants (and sometimes he does)." But no one there, and I mean no one, can look at him without bursting, literally bursting, into joy.

A CERTAIN MAN HAD TWO SONS

I think Jesus looks at us the same way. He just can't help himself. One way I know that is that he talks about it in scripture. It says, "A certain man had two sons." And the one son comes to his father and says, "I want my share of the inheritance." I can only imagine the sadness his father felt, not only that his son was willing to ask for "his share" at this point, but also knowing that he would take it and leave.

And leave he does, to a distant land where he squanders all he has with loose living. What a temptation that is. Not just for this young son but also for all of us—to rebel, to leave, to just chuck it all and go, to escape. And when you are feeling like he is almost any kind of sin will do . . . for a while.

FEEDING PIGS

But then the money runs out and this poor boy finds himself literally in a pigsty. For a young Jewish boy, there really couldn't be anything worse. Dirty. Unclean. Smelly. Disgusting. Miserable. And oh, was he hungry. He is so hungry the Bible says he longs to eat the slop he is feeding to the pigs.

At home on the farm, his father is heartbroken. He sits each evening out on the porch, looking out over the horizon. He waits and watches. He thinks of his son, how much he loves him, how he longs to see him and be with him, how he fears for his safety and wonders where he is and only wants him to come home. At night, when he sits down to dinner, he looks at his son's place, an empty seat, and as best he can, he holds on to hope. He walks into his room where he would tuck him in each night as a child and he prays and he wonders.

THAT'S MY BOY

And then one day, his father is out in the field working. It's getting late, almost quitting time, and out of the corner of his eye he catches a glimpse of a figure barely walking, bent over, tired, sad, broken, dirty, crushed under the weight of his own guilt and shame, this figure still a long way off.

"Are you serious? Can it be?" He has seen that gait before—

that stride, that frame, the sandy hair, the worn out ball cap. And he yells, "That's him! That's my boy! He's here! He's coming home!" And sure enough, he is.

The father runs. He runs with joy. He runs with truth. He runs with passion. He runs with love and mercy and forgiveness, his face exploding with excitement, every fiber, every cell, every part of his body, even his own soul, is celebrating.

He sees us when he's running. He sees you and me, broken by sin and hurt and pain, yet coming to our senses, turning around and coming home.

He runs and greets his boy, who with whatever pride he has left says, "Daddy, I have sinned and am no longer worthy to be called your son."

And his father, with his arms wrapped around him, holding his boys head to his chest, almost instantly interrupts and says, "Shhhhh, shhhhh . . . It is okay. It is okay." Then to the servants, "Get the best robe and put it on his back. Get the ring and put it on his finger. Get the sandals and put them on his feet, and go and kill the fatted calf, for this son of mine was dead and is now alive, he was lost and is now found."

And they have a party.

Not just any kind of party. This party goes on for days. I remember my grandmother telling me that when my mom and dad got married the last person left her house three days after the wedding. It was that kind of party. It was the whole town kind of party with music and dancing and food and drink and laughing and stories and singing. One flat out, big time, blow the top off, last one, turn off the lights celebration. God loves to celebrate. Especially when we come home. No matter where we've been. "So awesome. So great."

FULLY RESTORED, FULLY LOVED

There is so much I love about this story. I love the truth of rebellion and the fact that we all have literally run from our father. I love how it relays the pain of living in a "distant land" and how that kind of living is relentless in tearing down the soul. The utter despair of feeding pigs and how dirty and unworthy that must have made the son feel.

And yet, there is such great hope. A "coming to the senses," a waking up, God moving in the heart of this boy to know that he can go home, he has a father who loves him, who can and will restore him and restore him fully, put the best robe on his back, a ring on his finger, sandals on his feet, "for this son of mine was lost and now is found, he was dead and is now alive." Wow.

And then there is the party. "Go and fetch the fatted calf. Invite the entire town. We will have a feast. For my boy, the one I love, is home. He is home. And it is good."

LOVES US THIS MUCH

It is hard to imagine how different life would be if we lived like this—to know that God loves us this much. That he so much wants us home. He waits for us; he looks for us; he desires and wants, more than anything else, to be with us, to love us, and to restore us. And he celebrates us. His face lights up like David's does when he sees us. Each time I see David celebrate I am reminded of what God looks like when he looks at us.

He is so excited. He loses control. He runs to us. He throws his arms around us. He invites everyone over, and we kill the fatted calf. He says, "It's okay, I know. But you are not one of my hired men you are my son. You are my daughter. And it's okay. You are home now. And it is okay."

JOURNAL

Think about a time you felt lost, alone, shameful, and dirty, out feeding pigs. How did that feel? Where were you, and how did you get there?

_____

_____

_____

_____

_____

What would it mean to come to your senses, to go home, to find your Father?

_____

_____

_____

_____

_____

See him running to you; what does it feel like and look like as he is greeting you, throwing his arms around you? You hear his words, "This son of mine, this daughter of mine, was dead and is now alive. She was lost and now is found. So they began to celebrate."

_____

_____

_____

_____

_____

PRAY

Thank you, Jesus, for how much you love me even in the midst of my guilt and shame, how you desire me home, how you run to me, and how more than anything else you want to embrace me, tell me it's okay no matter where I've been or what I've done. I am yours, and you are mine. Thank you, Jesus.

10

Riding Tandem

*"Fan into flame the gift of God, which is in you
by the laying on of my hands" (II Timothy 1:6).*

READ

Psalm 86
II Timothy 1:1-7

SILENCE.

I heard it said once, "Whichever direction your relationship is heading, riding a tandem bike together will get it there faster." There could not be a statement truer.

David loves a bike. He likes to ride, and the faster the better. When he was small we had a Burleigh trailer that I used to strap him into. We would go to the park or to the pool or just on a long ride together.

When we moved to New York, David was getting too big for that trailer, so it was time to look into other options. A neighborhood bike shop sold a small bike that could attach to my mountain bike. As David likes to say, "Perfect."

THE PARK

So off we went, through Central Park, to the "big playground," weaving in and out between runners, walkers, skateboarders, and other cyclists. As one passerby said, "Crossing the street in Central Park on a warm Saturday afternoon is like a good game of Frogger, dude."

To ride tandem well, one has to lead and the other has to follow. There has to be a great deal of trust that the leader won't go too fast, drive recklessly, run into another cyclist, hit a tree, or slam into the curb.

Both cyclists have to work together, pedal together, lean in together, steer in the same general direction, and, hopefully, want to wind up in the same spot. This is the ultimate team sport, and if it is to be done well, it will require a little give on both parts.

David is a great partner. He loves riding together and rarely complains. He will go just about anywhere, and he loves being with his dad.

DAYDREAMS

He does daydream, which means we swerve a lot, which drives the serious cyclists in the park crazy. "Hold your line! . . . On your left!"

"Give me a stinkin' break! You try "holding your line" with a one-hundred-twenty-five-pound kid with Down syndrome on the back who is looking at birds and squirrels, riding with both feet out, waving at friends, and laughing at people as we pass them by. Try giving that a shot, Mr. Bike Gear, helmet head, Livestrong-bike-shorts, way-too-intense, no-room-for-silly, gotta-activate-my-inner-core, workout person!"

David also refuses to pedal. There are some great hills in the park that would be a great opportunity for some teamwork. As we start up, he can tell I'm struggling, and I'll yell, "Pedal, David!"

And he'll yell back, "No!" And then I feel him giggling. I look beside us and realize he's not the only one who thinks this is funny.

I am also stunned by how many people often pull up beside me and say, "He's not pedaling."

"Really? Thank you. I hadn't noticed. That's helpful."

FOLLOWING JESUS

Following Jesus often feels, to me, like riding tandem. I have to learn to trust. I have to be willing to follow. I have to want to work together. Jesus often says, "Pedal!" And I say, "No!" That's probably not good.

However, I am beginning to learn to enjoy the ride almost as much as David does. I have to challenge myself to ride with both feet out, to watch for the birds and squirrels, to wave at friends, and to try and not take too seriously those intense dudes in the bike shorts.

PAUL AND TIMOTHY

When I think of two men who rode tandem, I think of Paul and Timothy. Paul was such a great leader, such a great teacher, and such a passionate follower of Jesus. And he loved Timothy, which almost seems a prerequisite to riding tandem well.

Paul starts this second letter to Timothy saying, "Paul, an apostle of Christ Jesus by the will of God, according to the promise of life that is in Christ Jesus, To Timothy, my dear son."

Wow. My dear son. That is a whole lot deeper than a partner or even friend. There are very few bonds more profound than a father and a son.

He goes on to say, "Fan into flame the gift of God, which is in you by the laying on of my hands" (*v. 6*).

SCOTT

When I first came on the Young Life staff, I was young, just barely out of college, moving into the city, wet behind the ears as they say, and knew a whole lot less than I thought I knew.

Fortunately, I was not left alone. In God's great wisdom he paired me with Scott Dimock, an older, much wiser man, who had been on staff for close to twenty years at that point. Scott took the time to teach me. He encouraged me to use my unique talents, to develop my dependable strengths, to fan into flame the gifts God had given me, and then gave me room to fail. Failure is such a great teacher. But Scott would dust me off, love me through it, help me to process, listen to me, coach me, and encourage me to get back in there.

God is a God of relationships and a God of disciple making—whether it be the Father and Jesus or Jesus and the disciples or Barnabas and Paul or Moses and Joshua or Elijah and Elisha or Paul and Timothy or me and Scott. Learning to be on the back of the tandem is such an important part of learning what it means to love and follow Jesus.

CANYONLANDS

Riding tandem is not only fun, it also serves a great purpose. None of us who were around then would forget the story of

Aron Ralston, the guy in Utah who while hiking in Canyonlands National Park was pinned to the canyon wall by a boulder that was dislodged from above. He anguished there for six days before finally cutting off his own arm and walking out.

In an interview later, when asked what mistake he thought he had made that day he said, "I didn't tell anyone where I was or where I was going. No one knew where to find me." He nearly died.

Too many of us, as fellow believers, don't have someone in our lives who knows where we are—who really knows, who we are being completely honest with, who we are sharing life with. Unfortunately, way too many of us are riding solo.

Jesus said, "Greater love has no one than this: that he lay down his life for his friends" (*John 15:13*).

The best way I know to do that is to follow Jesus and to always ride tandem.

JOURNAL

What does it mean for you to ride tandem with someone in your life and ministry? What is hard about that? What is life giving? Reflect for a moment on whom you ride with when you are on the front of the bike and whom you ride with when you are on the second seat?

How did Paul and Timothy model this relationship? What difference did that make to each of them? How did Paul know what to do with Timothy, how to mold and shape him?

_____

_____

_____

_____

_____

What is Jesus saying to you about not being alone? Who is it that is *riding* with you? How can you be more intentional about that relationship?

_____

_____

_____

_____

_____

PRAY

Jesus, thank you that you don't ever want us to be completely alone. Thank you that you provide friends and partners and "sons" for us to "ride with." I pray for that person today, that I would take advantage of that relationship, that I would be intentional, that I would find time, that we would share life— both the uphills and downhills together—that we would pedal for each other, and that the ride would be that much sweeter because we are doing it together.

11

Carry You

*"Filled with compassion, Jesus reached out his hand
and touched the man" (Mark 1:41).*

READ

Psalm 62
Mark 1:40-45

SILENCE.

David hates to walk. Typically, and this was especially true when he was young, he would walk for maybe four-to-five blocks, then plop down in the middle of the sidewalk and say, "Carry you! Carry you!" (For some reason he would always get the you and me mixed up, but we certainly knew what he meant.)

When Jessi was with us, she was the best. She would crouch down in front of David and he would crawl up on her back and away they went. This went on until he was eleven or twelve, and maybe weighed almost as much as she did.

MY ROCK

There have been hundreds of times, more than I care to remember, that I have watched this scenario unfold and thought, *Man, would I like someone to carry me?*

Psalm 62 says, "Find rest, O my soul, in God alone; my hope comes from him. He alone is my rock and my salvation; he is my fortress, I will not be shaken" (*v. 5-6*).

I think of how many times over the years, when I couldn't make it another step, God has carried me. Times when I thought, *I am done, absolutely done,* and God has said, "Here, crawl up on my back. I am your rock. I am your fortress and your salvation. I will not be shaken."

A MAN WITH LEPROSY

Our story in *Mark 1* starts by saying, "A man with leprosy came to him and begged him on his knees." The Bible makes it clear this wasn't just any man, but a man with *leprosy.*

I am not sure there could have been anything much worse during that time period than having leprosy. It was an awful disease. It ate away your fingers, toes, parts of your face, ears, and nose. It produced boils and sores on the skin, lesions, hair loss—it was horrible, ugly, and grotesque.

Maybe worse was the fact that your community shunned you. Someone with leprosy was considered unclean (see *Leviticus 13)* and therefore wasn't welcome in worship. They would be isolated from friends and family, often living outside of town with other lepers, so they were denied contact with *normal* people. If they came into town, they often wore a bell around their neck, walked on the other side of the street, and were made to scream, "Unclean! Unclean!"

Lost, lonely, rejected, alone, and desperate this man lands on his knees at the feet of Jesus. Carry you.

IF YOU ARE WILLING

"If you are willing, you can make me clean," the man said. Wow.

We are still in the first chapter of *Mark,* but this man knows enough about Jesus to know that if he is willing, he can do this. Maybe he was in Capernaum when the "whole town gathered at the door and Jesus healed many with various diseases" (*Mark 1:33-34).*

Maybe he had just heard rumors. Maybe he overheard the disciples talking. In any event, he was confident that if Jesus wanted to, he could heal him.

FILLED WITH COMPASSION

The very next verse is one of my favorite verses in the Bible. It says, "Filled with compassion, Jesus . . ." Filled with compassion! When Jesus looked at this guy, you know what he saw? He saw you and me. He saw a guy that had been created in his image, in the image of God. A guy whose life had dealt him some pretty tough blows, who was lonely, who was afraid, and who was desperate—Jesus looked at him and he loved him!

Then it says, "Jesus reached out his hand and he touched him" (*v. 41*).

Do you know when the last time this guy had anyone touch him? You know how good that feels—when someone puts their arm around you, grabs your hand, puts a hand on your shoulder, or bends down low enough and lets you crawl up on their back?

INTENTIONAL

Jesus is God of the Universe. He could have done this any way he wanted. He could have simply said, "Okay, I'll do that. I can make you clean. Just move back a bit." Or he could have healed him and then gone over and hugged him. Or he could have asked one of the disciples to simply put a hand on him while he healed him. But he didn't. While he was still *sick*, still *contagious*, still *unclean*, and still *unwanted* Jesus put his arm around him. And then he healed him.

Jesus is intentional. There is very little wasted effort. Jesus did this with purpose. There is power in that touch. It was as if he was saying, "You matter to me. You are important. You are a person, with a name and a story. You are not a disease. You are not invisible. You are a child of God. You are created in my image. You have dignity. Your life matters to me, and I am going to prove it to you."

ROPES COURSE

One of my first opportunities to be at Capernaum camp, which at the time was maybe one hundred fifty kids with disabilities and their buddies and leaders, was at Crooked Creek in Colorado. At the time, different than we would do at a typical week of camp, the entire camp did the ropes course on the same day.

(The ropes course is an obstacle course maybe thirty-five to forty feet in the air with twelve to fifteen different obstacles that generally ends in a giant swing or a zip line back down to the ground.)

So instead of a few kids under the ropes course cheering kids on, there were maybe two hundred fifty. It was an incredible sight. The goal was to get every kid in camp through on the same day, or at least to give them the opportunity.

Most of these kids, especially at the beginning of the day, were physically able. Some of them zoomed through. There was lots of laughter and cheers, high fives, leaders laughing with kids, hugs, and then more cheers. It was great.

And then we got to Edward.

EDWARD

Edward was in a wheelchair and had cerebral palsy. He couldn't walk, had limited use of his hands, and was nonverbal. The word *profound* might be used with Edward.

I fully expected Edward's leader to explain to him why this wouldn't work so well and why we would cheer for him perhaps, but he couldn't or wouldn't be able to do the ropes course.

But that wasn't what anyone was thinking, most especially Edward and Edward's leader. "You can do this Edward!" his leader screamed as they hoisted Edward out of his chair and up onto the course. "You can do this!"

I am thinking, *Are they kidding? This is crazy.*

For two hours Edward pulled, pushed, struggled, grunted, and even cried. Places where he would stop and knew he just couldn't make it another step, his leader came over, knelt down, and Edward crawled up on his back and he carried him through.

As Edward came closer to the finish, the crowd began to roar. "Go, Edward, you got this! You got this, Edward." His leader was exhausted. He was soaked in sweat. His hands trembled on the rope.

They came to the last element. Together with tears streaming down their faces, Edward and his leader zip lined back to the ground. The whole place went bananas with cheers, high fives, and double high fives. Everyone went absolutely nuts.

I smiled. And through the tears and high fives I thought, *Dignity. This kid matters.* David matters. You matter.

Jesus said, "I am willing. Be clean." And the Bible says, "Immediately, the leprosy left him and he was cured" (*Mark 1:42*).

JOURNAL

Think of a time in your life when you felt like you just couldn't push through, where you knew you needed help, where you simply felt like sitting on the ground, throwing your arms up in the air, and saying, "Carry me!"

_____

_____

_____

_____

_____

How does the man in the story come to Jesus? What is he feeling and hoping? How does Jesus react to him? What were people in the crowd thinking as they saw this?

_____

_____

_____

_____

_____

How does Jesus see you? How is he willing to enter in, to put an arm around you? How does Jesus see people who might be different than you?

_____

_____

_____

_____

_____

PRAYER

Thank you, dear Jesus, for how you see us, how you stop for us, how you are willing, how you enter in, how the intimacy of your touch says we matter. Thank you for how you give us dignity, how you have the power to not only heal us but to make us whole, to make us clean. Thank you, dear Jesus.

12

My Daddy

"Very early in the morning, while it was still dark, Jesus got up, left the house and went to a solitary place, where he prayed"
(Mark 1:35).

READ

Psalm 103
Mark 1:29-39

SILENCE.

I love the fact that every once in a while David will look up at me and say, "My daddy." There is a certain childlike quality to it, a recognition, an intimacy, a sense of gratitude, a genuine love—a real sense that he is not only saying, "My daddy," but also, "I am so glad that you are my daddy."

And I am so glad that I am his daddy, that I know him, that I get to hang out with him, that we spend lots of time together, and that he and I just enjoy being together: playing, laughing, eating, watching baseball, riding bikes, kayaking, or just hanging out.

SARANAC

We just got back from a weekend together at Saranac Lake, our Young Life camp in the Adirondacks. It was so great. We tubed together. We went down the slide together. We ate together. We laughed. We hugged. We hung out. We stayed in the same room. It was great.

Every once in a while, when our kids were young, they would simply crawl up in my lap and sit there. It was a chance to get a little daddy time. We didn't say much. We simply snuggled. But it was so great. I got home from a trip a couple of days ago, and David just came over and laid down in my lap. Not next to me. On top of me.

Our world is so crazy busy. Daddy time is hard to find.

Psalm 103 says, "For as high as the heavens are above the earth, so great is his love toward those who fear him; as far as the east is from the west, so far has he removed our transgressions from us. As a father has compassion on his children, so the Lord has compassion on those who fear him" (*v. 11-13*).

CRAZY IN LOVE

I just love that picture of a Father who is crazy in love with his kids, who doesn't really want anything from them, who knows they can't earn it, and who simply lavishes his love on them because they are his kids and really for no other reason. At the end of the day, when it is all said and done, he really just wants to be with them.

One of the unintended consequences, in my opinion, of our fast-paced, distracted, cell phone, texting, tweeting culture is that we have lost some of the intimacy of personal face-to-face interaction. A tweet just isn't as good as a hug. A text just isn't the same as a kiss on the cheek or a warm embrace. A long post doesn't satisfy like a long, intimate conversation. Something feels lost there. What at one time seemed somewhat slow and deep, now feels very fast and shallow.

DADDY TIME

Jesus loved daddy time. It was a gift. He loved the silence. It was his time to pray, to cultivate, to listen, to wait, to be available, to detach from the noise and hustle of life in the crowds, to disconnect in order to reconnect, and to simply rest and allow his daddy to love him.

VERY EARLY IN THE MORNING

One of my favorite stories of him doing that is in *Mark 1*. The evening prior he had worked well into the night. The Bible says, "After sunset the people brought to Jesus all the sick and demon-possessed. The "whole town gathered at the door" (*v. 32-33*). Can you imagine the whole town? Can you see Peter peaking out the front door saying, "Hey guys, look at this, the whole town is out here?"

And then the next paragraph starts, "Very early in the morning, while it was still dark, Jesus got up, left the house and went off to a solitary place, where he prayed" (*v. 35*). I love that verse. "Very early." He had to have been up late the night before. He had to have been tired from being with people, healing the sick, and casting out the demons. Exhausted. "Let's sleep in." Nope. "Let's get up early." Why? So that he could go to a solitary place and be with dad, to listen to the Father, and to refill, restore, recreate, and reload. Snuggle time.

SOMEWHERE ELSE

And then a great thing happens. Simon gathers a posse and goes to look for him. And the Bible says, "When they found him, they exclaimed, 'Everyone is looking for you!'"

Simon seemed almost a little perturbed, like what are you doing out here? Everyone is looking for you. We got things to do. People are waiting! We have momentum! This is your big chance! Maybe more importantly, this is our big chance!

I love this. Jesus replied, "Let us go somewhere else—to nearby villages—so I can preach there also. That is why I have come." Somewhere else! Where is somewhere else? Why are we going there? Everyone is here. And they are waiting. They are waiting for you to show up. Why are we going somewhere else?

IN THE CROWD

You know, in the crowd, in the constant drive and hustle of everyday life, it is just hard to hear. It's almost impossible. If Jesus sleeps in that morning, he probably doesn't move. Why would he? Everyone is there and waiting for him.

But as he is alone, as he sits in quiet, in solitude, he begins to hear, and to hear clearly, the Father's voice. "You need to get up. You need to go to the other villages. For that is why you have come."

The next three stories are about him with a leper and then the paralytic being lowered through the roof and then his encounter with Levi aside the lake. I wonder how many of those would have never happened if he had just stayed where he was, if he hadn't taken time to be alone and listen that morning?

EARLY IN THE MORNING

Over the course of the last thirty years, my early mornings have become precious to me. Now that David is getting up early to go to school, I get up earlier and earlier. Sometimes I walk, sometimes I sit out back behind our apartment, sometimes I sit in the dark of our living room—but I sit and I am still and I listen.

When I first came on the Young Life staff, I spent a month at what we called the Young Life Institute. There I met Tom Raley, who was a long-time veteran staff person and was serving alongside of his wife, Recie, as the chaplains for the month. Tom talked about these "days away" that he spent with Jesus, days where he would go to a lonely place and spend the entire day in solitude with Jesus. I remember thinking, *Are you kidding me? The whole day?*

But then I tried it. That was close to thirty years ago. I think that one discipline, that one event of every month taking a day and going to a lonely place, has allowed me to stay in ministry all these years. There were days as a young staff person when I wanted to quit, days when it just wasn't working out, days when I knew I didn't have the gifts or the smarts or charisma or whatever it takes, days when I wanted, actually begged the Lord, to let me go and let me do something else, and I would go and be alone, quiet, still, and let Jesus love me, hug me, lead me, and speak to me. I was having daddy time.

DAYSPRING

When we lived in Gaithersburg we lived fifteen minutes from Dayspring, a place founded by the Church of the Savior and dedicated as a place of silence and retreat. I went there every month for ten years straight. I know animals that live on that property by name. I have trees that slap me high five when I show up. There is a bench by a pond there that has the curvature of my bottom on it because I spent so many hours sitting there.

I would meet with my spiritual director at 9 a.m. for an hour. She would listen to me, pray for me, give me something to read or think about, and then send me on my way. I still think often of our times together.

IN THE GARDEN

At the end of his life, Jesus finds himself alone again in a garden. Now the battle is raging— on the outside certainly but, more importantly, in his heart and in his soul. He begs three times for the Father to take this cup from him. His disciples, who over and over he encouraged to stay up and pray with him, have fallen asleep. He battles with his own fear, pain, anguish, doubt, desire—his human flesh rages against his soul. Our souls and the future of all mankind hang in the balance.

And his Father is close, and he knows he's close because he is accustomed to being alone with his Father. And it's okay. And his Father speaks, and Jesus hears him because he knows his voice. The time comes and he is ready, and he gets up, walks out of the garden, down the hill, and to the cross.

JOURNAL

Think of the daddy time you had with your dad growing up, or maybe with your own children. What was that like? Where did you go? What did you do? (Not all of us had that kind of intimate one-on-one time, and it is okay to acknowledge that and process it.)

_____

_____

_____

_____

_____

Think of Jesus, what do you think his relationship was like with his Daddy? Where else do you see him alone with the Father (*Matt. 14, John 17*)? What do you think those times looked like?

_____

_____

_____

_____

_____

What are your times like alone with Jesus? How do you make room and time to be still, to listen, and to turn down the volume to allow Jesus to speak? What impact do those times have on the rest of your day?

_____

_____

_____

_____

_____

PRAYER

Jesus, thank you for those alone times that you had with your Daddy, places where you retreated from the crowd and the noise, where you sat in silence, where you listened, waited, and asked, and where you were held and hugged and you just allowed your Father to love you. Help me to find those places, to have the courage, to find the time—to go, to wait, to be still, and to listen. Speak, Lord Jesus.

13

Breathe In,
Breathe Out

"Jesus came and stood among them and said,
'Peace be with you'" (John 20:19).

READ

Psalm 30
John 11:17-44

SILENCE.

I was headed to the high school. It was Friday night and there was a football game. My daughter, Jessi, was already there. She was a freshmen and this was her first real high school game.

My phone rang. It was one of the administrators from the school.

She said, "Mr. Wagner?"

"Yes," I answered.

"This is Ms. Jones from Quince Orchard High School. You need to get here right away. Your daughter is having a medical emergency."

A what? What does that mean? I floored it. My mind and my head started racing. What is going on? Why did she say that? What possible *emergency* could Jessi be having?

I cut through the parking lot off of Route 28 and parked behind the Dunkin Donuts. Michael was with me. I could already see the lights of the ambulance across the way. I got out of my car and ran. Jessi was on a stretcher and being loaded into the back of the ambulance. She had had a seizure.

CRAZY THINGS

All kinds of crazy things now are going through my head. There is a huge crowd watching. Hardly anyone is paying attention to the game. The school administrator who called is now asking me questions. She sounds like the teacher on Charlie Brown. I am looking at her. I can hear her. But nothing makes sense.

I run back to my car, jump in, and follow the ambulance to the hospital, thinking, *What in the world could all of this mean? Why did Jessi have a seizure? Brain tumor? Epilepsy? Who has seizures? Now what? How are we going to deal with this? What is going to happen with my baby?*

I get to the hospital and run from the car. Gae is there now and we both watch as they wheel Jessi into the emergency room. She is conscious, but barely. There is a mask on her face so she can't talk. Gae and I hold hands.

After a couple hours of examination, the doctor basically tells us, "She seems fine. I don't see anything wrong. You can go home."

AGAIN

It was a huge relief until the following week when it happened again and then a couple of weeks later when it happened again. We started seeing specialist after specialist and neurologists and neuro-psychs and psychologists, and no one could tell us what was wrong.

This literally went on for the next couple of years. And in the middle of it there were deep times and places of darkness and despair for Gae and me. I am not sure where he learned it or who taught it to him, but David, who was eleven at the time, started doing this thing where he would look at us and say, "Breathe in, breathe out." He even had the hand motions where he would put his hands out and then bring them in to his mouth and then back out again.

It cracked Gae and me up every time. We needed it. It got to a point where we were saying it to each other. "Breathe in, breathe out." I still say it today.

LAZARUS

When I think of that time, I often think of the story of Lazarus in *John 11*. Jesus had received word that Lazarus was sick. The Bible doesn't tell us how he was sick, but he was sick enough that Mary and Martha thought they should contact Jesus and tell him to come at once.

He didn't. He waited.

Jesus says just before, "This sickness will not end in death. No, it is for God's glory so that God's Son may be glorified through it" (*v. 4*). Well, sure, but Mary and Martha don't know that. What they know is that their brother is lying there dying, and Jesus is not showing up.

CHARLESTON

At one point in this journey with Jessi we were in Charleston, South Carolina dropping Michael off for his first year at the College of Charleston. There is a large bridge there that spans the Cooper River. Jessi was not doing particularly well that weekend. I remember telling Gae that I was going out for a run.

I got to that bridge and it just started flowing out of me. "What makes you think I can handle this, Lord? Where are you? When are you going to show up? Why not take me instead? Is this some kind of cruel punishment? Have I done something to offend you? Is this an attack of the enemy? Are you trying to tell me something? Where in the hell are you? Why aren't you listening to me!"

Tears flowed. I'd been holding it in for so long. Too long.

JESUS

Lazarus dies. Tears flow. And Jesus still has not shown up.

When Jesus finally does, Martha has come unhinged. She goes out to meet him and says, "Lord, if you had been here, my brother would not have died." Basically she says, "Where have you been? Oh, and what took you so long? Did you get our message?"

And then she gathers herself and says, "But I know even now God will give you whatever you ask."

"I am the resurrection and the life," Jesus says. "He who believes in me will live, even though he dies, and whoever lives in me will never die. Do you believe this?" It is the simple but powerful truth of the gospel. "Breathe in, breathe out."

"Yes, Lord," she told him, "I believe that you are the Christ, the Son of God, who was to come into the world."

Martha had to answer this question: "Now that your brother is dead, is Jesus still Lord, is he still the Christ, the Son of the Living God?"

When Jessi was really sick I had to ask myself, "Do you still believe I am who I said I am? Am I Lord and God or aren't I? Am I still in control? Or is it only when things are going like you had hoped?"

JESUS

"Jesus wept." He broke. He couldn't hold it anymore. He loved this family. He loved Lazarus. He loved Mary and Martha. He had been holding it in a long time. Too long.

Then it says, "Once more deeply moved"—I love how human he is—"Jesus called in a loud voice, 'Lazarus come out.'"

Bob Mitchell, former president of Young Life, used to say, "I am glad he called him by name. Apparently, there were a lot of bodies in there." I love Bob.

The Bible says, "The dead man came out, his hands and feet wrapped with strips of linen, and a cloth around his face." How would you have liked to have been there that day? How would you have liked to be Mary or Martha? Their brother was alive after being dead for four days. If that didn't blow your mind, nothing would have.

"Take off the grave clothes and let him go." So that God might be glorified.

"Breathe in, breathe out."

JOURNAL

Think of a time in your life when you felt most desperate, out of control, unable to make sense of what was happening. How did that feel?

_____

_____

_____

_____

_____

How does Jesus show up in this story? How did he show up in yours? What changed when Jesus showed up? How long did that change last?

_____

_____

_____

_____

_____

How do we learn to trust Jesus in the midst of what seems most desperate and hopeless?

_____

_____

_____

_____

_____

PRAY

Thank you, God, in the midst of what feels so dark and hopeless, you are there, you are with us, you hear us, and you know how we feel and where we hurt. We are confident that you are good. You are good and powerful and able to make things new. We believe that today. We believe it.

14

Sorry

'No one, sir,' she said.
'Then neither do I condemn you,' Jesus declared
(John 8:11).

READ

Psalm 51
John 8:1-11

SILENCE.

Ever since I was a little boy, our family spent our spring breaks in Florida. My grandfather was a fisherman, so as soon as he was able, he, along with my grandmother, found himself a small place in the Florida Keys, set up shop, and started fishing. We would go every year, my parents, my sister, my brother, and me, and the seven of us would crowd into a two-bedroom house. And we would have a blast.

GO DAY

The wind played a major role as to whether or not we could get out to fish on any given day. The best fishing was maybe six miles offshore on the ocean side. He didn't have a huge boat, so it had to be fairly calm for us to be able to go.

If the wind were to settle though, he would come shake us early and say, "It's a go day!" Wow. Those words still give me goose bumps. And my brother, sister, and I would jump out of bed, throw on our shorts, and we were out the door.

"Maybe this would be the day I will catch a barracuda or a Spanish mackerel or a huge grouper or a sail fish or, heaven forbid, a hammerhead shark!"

Some forty years later, that tradition continues. My grandfather has passed now, so we don't always go to the Keys.

But we always go to Florida. This past year we went to Marco Island, just below Naples, and met my parents and my brother and his family. It's really too far to drive with David, so typically we fly.

SLIGHT DELAY

This particular time, we had a slight delay coming out of LaGuardia because of weather around the Ft. Myers airport. Gae is always prepared with snacks and fresh things to eat, so David sat quietly in the terminal munching on carrots and ranch dressing. I know. He loves it. That's what he gets for growing up in our family. Poor kid has never seen a donut.

Finally, it was time to board. Apparently, there were still thunderstorms in the Ft. Myers area, but there was a small window and if we could get moving we could get there and land safely. So, as we often try to do, we get bulkhead seats so David isn't kicking the person in front of him or pushing on his seat. We got on and we buckled in.

The trip down was delightful. David watched his iPad. Had another snack. Gae and I read a bit. I napped, which is rare, I know, especially on a plane. And then we began our descent into Ft. Myers.

It was cloudy and obviously going to be bumpy. The captain came on the radio and said, "We need everyone in their seats and buckled immediately. Flight attendants, please take your seats." I could feel the tension.

BOUNCE

As soon as he was done saying that the plane begins to bounce. And we are going up and down, like we just came out of shoot #7 riding HotDang. And people in the back are yelling. And you hear a few drinks hit the floor. And Gae has dug her fingernails into my forearm and is clutching on for dear life. And the flight attendant looks like this might be her first rodeo. And I look over at David, and I can see him just going up and down, up over the wave and back down again, holding on.

Finally, the landing gear is down, and we can't be more than fifteen feet from the ground, and we think we are going to make it. The wind is blowing and the rain is driving. My shirt is soaked through with sweat, and Gae hasn't opened her eyes in maybe twenty minutes. The wheels finally hit the ground and people cheer, the flight attendant exhales, Gae lets go of my arm, and out of what seems like nowhere . . . David blows lunch. I mean projectile. Full force. Yellow like a big whopping bucket of yellow goo running down the wall of the bulkhead. I mean, "Wow, that's incredible."

And as the plane begins to come to a slow coast along the runway the flight attendant starts throwing me wet towels, and people are excusing themselves and fixing their hair, trying not to look over at us but not being able to help themselves. David looks over at Gae and says, "Too many carrots, Mommy. Too many carrots. I'm sorry."

Oh man. That is such a sweet boy.

I'M SORRY

There is something deeply refreshing about saying, "I'm sorry." There is something healthy and healing about it, something that says, "I'm not perfect. I make mistakes. I do things that sometimes hurt me or hurt others, and I'm sorry about that." For David that is just second nature. Even when it isn't his fault.

Paul says in *Romans 7* that he "does the things that he doesn't want to do and doesn't do the things he should do" (*v. 15*). This is coming from a guy who started over a dozen churches, preached the Gospel in most of the Gentile world, and wrote two-thirds of the New Testament. What does he have to be sorry about?

I love the fact that we "confess our sins" every Sunday in our church, often on our knees. We say:

> *Most merciful God,*
> *we confess that we have sinned against you*
> *in thought, word, and deed*
> *by what we have done and by what we have left undone.*
> *We have not loved you with our whole heart and*
> *we have not loved our neighbors as ourselves.*
> *We are truly sorry and we humbly repent . . .*
> *Have mercy on us and forgive us.*

That is a prayer that has been said for hundreds, if not thousands, of years in churches around the world. It is saying we are sorry. It is we together, as a community, simply being honest.

At the deepest and most central part of the gospel is this sense of forgiveness and mercy, this admission of guilt and the great pardon of the cross. In our Lord's Prayer, which we also say every week, we say, "Forgive us our debts as we forgive our debtors." I am fairly certain God hears all those prayers

CAUGHT IN ADULTERY

In our gospel story today, Jesus is again teaching in the temple. It is just after dawn, and it says, "All the people gathered around him," as they often did. And he spoke to them the words of life.

It goes on to say that the Pharisees and teachers of the law brought a woman caught in adultery and made her stand in front of the group—half dressed, naked, embarrassed, humiliated, guilty, filled with shame, and now brought in front of Jesus and the crowd and accused of a heinous sin.

"Teacher, this woman was caught in the act of adultery (in "the act" so, obviously, there had to be a man present when they found her). In the Law, Moses commanded us to stone such women. Now what do you say?"

Now there's a tight spot for you: The Pharisees, teachers of the law, who together were a fairly well respected lot by most; a crowd of people who can't wait to hear how Jesus handles this one; this woman—who had been caught in the act and appears for all intents and purposes to be guilty; and maybe a few of your own disciples standing by, who at this point are of no help, simply looking at each other and at their shoes. And now, all eyes are on you.

STOOPS DOWN

Jesus stoops down and writes on the ground. He crouches down and with his index finger begins to write in the dirt. Can you believe that? He just stays there. Doesn't say a word. Maybe he drew a cross. Maybe he wrote the word *mercy*. Maybe he wrote her name. Maybe he thought, "I love her enough, that I will soon die for her." Maybe he simply wrote: "I'm sorry."

At this point, you can cut the tension with a knife. People are anxiously waiting. A crowd of people, the disciples, the scribes and teachers of the law, and the woman are all standing there. The attention drifts off of her and on to him.

The Pharisees continue to question him, "What do you say? What do you say, Jesus?"

Again, he pauses. And finally, he straightens up and says, "If any one of you is without sin, let him be the first to throw a stone at her." And he stoops down again and writes on the ground.

"And at this they began to go away, one at a time, the older ones first, until it was just Jesus left there with the woman." Real truth. Real honesty. Real confession.

NO ONE CONDEMNS

"Woman, where are they? Has no one condemned you?"

"No one, sir."

"Then neither do I condemn you," Jesus declared. "Go now and leave your life of sin."

Unbelievable. No punishment. No guilt. No shame. No payment. She was guilty! She was caught in the act! She's a sinner! She has no defense! She didn't say a word. Everyone knew she was guilty.

And she was forgiven completely and without question. Even before she could say, "I'm sorry."

"Neither do I condemn you."

Complete, full, unmerited, undeserved, unearned, perhaps even completely unexpected, free, but very costly grace. Grace that only God can give.

JOURNAL

Think of a time you were caught red-handed, doing something you knew was wrong, and you were caught in the act? How did it feel? What was said to you? How did you react?

_____

_____

_____

_____

_____

What happens to this woman? How do you think she is feeling? How does Jesus respond? How do you think she is feeling as she leaves there?

_____

_____

_____

_____

_____

How about you, how do you experience God's forgiveness? Reflect for a moment on what Jesus did for you on the cross. How do you respond to him? What do you want to say to him?

_____

_____

_____

_____

_____

PRAY

Dear Jesus, today we do confess we have not loved you with our whole hearts. We have not loved our neighbors as ourselves. We are sorry and we humbly repent. Have mercy on us and forgive us. We are grateful today, Jesus, for your mercy and grace. Thank you for how much you love us.

15

Wonder and Awe

"They were terrified and asked each other, 'Who is this? Even the winds and waves obey him!'" (Mark 4:41).

READ

Psalm 143
Mark 4:35-41

SILENCE.

The other day, David and I were decorating the Christmas tree together. I have decorated our Christmas tree in one way or another for the last thirty years. David has helped.

For the most part, we have had the same ornaments for the better part of thirty years. I have seen them all, over and over. So has David.

Needless to say, opening the ornaments and putting them on the tree has become somewhat routine for me, but not for David. He loves it. He opens up an ornament with a picture of Michael on it when Michael was a baby and his face lights up, and he screams, "Michael!"

And I say, "Yes, David, that is Michael."

And then he sees the one that looks like the Nutcracker and he says, "Oooh, Daddy, what's this?"

And I say, "That's the Nutcracker, David."

And he says, "What's the Nutcracker about?"

And I say, "The Nutcracker is about a very pretty dance and a little girl and the Sugar Plum Fairy."

And he says, "Ooooh, I like the Nutcracker."

He picks another one that is the shape of Texas (nearly half of the ornaments in our house are either cows or cowboy boots or belt buckles or armadillos, not kidding). "What's this, Daddy?"

"It's Texas, David."

"Ewww, I love Texas."

You look at that boys face and there is sheer delight. It is the face of a child. It is the face of wonder. He is wrapped in magic and mystery. He really knows almost no theology around the miracle of Christmas. He couldn't tell you the first thing of the Trinity or of Incarnation or Christology or the Messiah or Covenant Theology. He is completely childlike—amazed, captivated, and filled with imagination, wonder, delight, and thoughts of things utterly impossible.

THAT DAY WHEN EVENING CAME

It is hard to imagine what it would have been like to have been one of the first disciples, to wake each morning wondering, "What unbelievable, crazy thing will happen today? Will Jesus heal another blind man or put his arms around a leper? Will we feed another five thousand people or cast demons out of guy in a cemetery or change water into wine or haul in a load of fish big enough to make the boat sink?"

There is a great story of the disciples with Jesus in *Mark 4*. It starts, "That day when evening came . . . " I often wonder why Jesus waited to start these traverses across the lake until evening. Isn't that something you would want to do in the morning, in broad daylight? These guys have little in the way of navigation systems, other than perhaps the stars. No GPS, no depth finders, no spotlight, no radio, nothing that we would take for granted on most sea-going vessels today, plus, its dark out there, which can't be good.

But Jesus says, "Let's go over to the other side." So they "leave the crowd behind" and take Jesus along "just as he was." What does that mean? They didn't ask him to change before he got in the boat?

Peter was thinking to himself, "I wouldn't wear those pants in the boat. But, hey, let's go. Just get in. It's gettin' late."

So off they go. And as it is like to do on the Sea of Galilee, especially, it seems, whenever the disciples are rowing hard toward the other side, a storm comes up. And it's not just a little storm. A "furious squall" says *Mark*, with gale force winds. A real "bottom buster," as my grandfather would like to say.

WAVES POUNDING

And the waves start pounding over the boat. So much so that

"it was nearly swamped," *Mark* says. I've been on a few boats that took waves over the bow, and it is scary. But then when you think these guys are rowing, there is no engine involved here; they could be miles from shore; most of them don't swim; there are no lifejackets; it's getting dark; the water is sloshing around your ankles; another breaker comes over the bow—and you are now in flat out panic.

And you look in the back of the boat wondering, "Hey, what happened to Jesus!" You don't see him anywhere. You shield your eyes from the spray, straining to see. And out of the corner of your eye, as another wave is breaking across the bow, choking salt water stinging your eyes, you see Jesus . . . Asleep! He's asleep! He's napping. He's out. He found a boat cushion, lay down, closed his eyes, and fell out.

You're joking. You are kidding me. You can't freakin' believe it. How can he sleep through this? We are dying out here. So you drop the oar, run to the back of the boat, grab him by the shirt collar, and say, "Hey, don't you care if we drown out here!" How many times have I wondered, in the midst of one of my own driving storms, with wind whipping across the bow, water hitting me in the face, if Jesus had just fallen asleep somewhere. Don't you care! Where are you? Can't you see I need help? I'm about to go down out here!

BE STILL!

He gets up and looks out over the raging water and yells, "Quiet! Be still!" Lord of all Creation. Then the wind died down and it was completely calm.

He looks at the disciples and says, "Why are you so afraid? Do you still have no faith?" Oh man. I'm feeling pretty bad right about now.

"Sorry, Jesus. Sorry to wake you. Matthew said I should."

The other guys in the back of the boat are whispering, "Did you see that? That was incredible. He just told the wind to stop it."

And the Bible says, "They were terrified."

ROUTINE

Sometimes I wonder, after forty years of walking with Jesus, if my life has just gotten a bit too routine, a bit too safe. When was the last time I was *terrified*? When was the last time I just sat in wonder? When was the last time I got to the end of something and thought, "Oh, wow, that was nuts!"

THE FIRST CHRISTMAS

On that very first Christmas, long before we had ornaments or the Nutcracker, it says there were "shepherds in the field, watching their flocks by night." An angel appeared to them and said, "Do not be afraid, I bring you good news of great joy that will be for all people. Today, in the town of David a Savior has been born to you, he is Christ the Lord."

A great company of heavenly hosts appeared glorifying and praising God saying, "Glory to God in the highest and on earth, peace to men on whom his favor rests."

And the shepherds went to Bethlehem and they saw Jesus and they found Mary and Joseph and the baby lying in a manger. They told them what the angel had said about this baby, and they were amazed.

They told others there in Bethlehem and they were amazed. Mary was also amazed and treasured these things in her heart, and the shepherds, who probably knew very little theology or Christology and maybe had never been to church, "returned glorifying and praising God for all the things they had heard and seen" (*Luke 2:20*). David would have loved being there that night.

It was a night of complete wonder and awe.

JOURNAL:

How has your life with Jesus become routine? Do you remember back to maybe earlier days or a time when that wasn't the case, when you sat in wonder and awe (and were maybe terrified) at something Jesus had done?

_____

_____

_____

_____

_____

How about the disciples, would any of their days with Jesus be seen as routine? The people who encounter Jesus, outside of the disciples, what is typically their reaction? Are they frightened? Angry? Hostile? Bored?

_____

_____

_____

_____

_____

How would life for you (and me) be different if each day we were encountering and walking with the authentic Jesus, this one who calmed the storms, who caused others to be terrified or amazed or in awe, who others worshipped or sat in wonder of or fell on their knees in his presence, that Jesus?

_____

_____

_____

_____

_____

PRAY

Help me, Jesus, that I might worship you, see you, and be awestruck by you. That I would live this day with expectant wonder saying, "What crazy thing will you do today? What crazy adventure will you take me on? Who will I meet? What miracle will I be in the middle of? How will you ask me to trust you more deeply? What risk will I take?" Help me to have dangerous faith today as I follow you.

16

Love You More

"Therefore, I tell you, her many sins have been forgiven
—for she loved much" (Luke 7:47).

READ

Psalm 130
Luke 7:36-50

SILENCE.

I am not sure where it started, maybe that kids' book *I Love you Bunches* or the Beatles hit song "She Loves You (Yeah, yeah, yeah)," but David will often say to Jessi, "Love you," and Jessi will respond, "Love you more," and David will say, "No, I love you more," and Jessi will say, "You more," then David, "No, you more," then Jessi, "You more," and they will go back and forth until they start tickling each other and David wets his pants.

I think of things I love: my wife, my kids, my folks, my family, friends, this Young Life mission, baseball, sports, being outside, going out to dinner, a good movie—some of it has to do with just who that person is, as in she's my wife or she's my daughter or he's my son. In other cases, it has more to do with what that person has done, how they've loved me or stuck with me or been there for me—in essence, I love them, because they first loved me.

When I think of David, I think of a boy who love just gushes out of, out of every pore of his being. He really just can't help himself. There is nothing he wants more than to be with you, to go on a walk with you, a bike ride, go to the park, swing, hang out, eat. He loves first.

Not so long ago, David and I had this wooden marble toy with ramps and swirlie things that we would play with for hours some afternoons in our basement (usually while I was watching a football game). He could play with that thing forever. It really didn't matter what you were doing. He just wanted to be with you.

WHAT A SCENE

I think of this woman. What a scene. Jesus is at the home of Simon, a well-known Pharisee. It is a dinner party, a dinner party consisting of all self-respecting men. Women were obviously not invited, especially not this type of woman.

The Bible is pretty clear. She is not just any woman. She is a *sinner*. She is a woman of the city. In more common language, she is most likely a prostitute. She is the least likely person to show up that night. She came knowing that she would most certainly be ridiculed, disrespected, embarrassed, and treated with contempt. She was, to put it mildly, *unwelcome*.

And yet she came anyway. Not only did she come but she also brought an alabaster jar of perfume, and she began to anoint the feet of Jesus. She began to weep and as she did the tears rolled down her cheeks and fell on Jesus's feet. She wiped them with her hair. She kissed them and caressed them. Love began to ooze out of every pore of her being.

Simon, watching this scene, began to think to himself, "If this were a prophet, he would know who is touching him and what kind of woman she is—that she is a sinner." What Simon doesn't realize is that Jesus knows exactly what he's thinking even without him saying it. Simon despised this woman and anyone like her and it was obvious.

DIGNITY AND RESPECT

Jesus first tells him a parable, the parable of the two debtors. And then, and I love this, the Bible says, "He turned to the woman and said to Simon." So he's looking at the woman, not at Simon—and by so doing, he's saying to her, "I see you; you have value, you have dignity, you have worth. I recognize your courage and how hard it was for you to come here tonight. I know you love me, and I receive your love. I will protect you. You are important, and you are forgiven."

Then he gives it to Simon. He says, "Do you see this woman?"

Fact is, he saw her and he judged her. He wanted nothing to do with her. She embarrassed him, and he thought Jesus should be embarrassed as well.

"You did not give me any water for my feet, but she wet my feet with her tears and wiped them with her hair. You did not give me a kiss, but this woman, from the time I entered, has not stopped kissing my feet. You did not put oil on my head, but she has poured perfume on my feet. Therefore, I tell you, her many sins have been forgiven—for she loved much. But he who has been forgiven little loves little" (*v. 44-47*).

Wow. It wasn't that Simon hadn't sinned much. He had sinned plenty. It was more that he hadn't been forgiven much. He hadn't allowed himself to be forgiven, to be loved by Jesus, to be undone by Jesus, to fully embrace the great love and compassion Jesus has for him.

Simon was prideful. He was arrogant and scornful. He was more concerned about doing things right, being good, earning it, keeping the rules, and managing an image. In his world it was pretty simple—he was *right*, and she was *wrong*. He was *good*, and she was *bad*. He was *religious*, and she was *sinful*.

RECKLESS PASSION

Who was this woman, and why did she show up that night? She was a sinner but not just any sinner. She was one who had been with Jesus. Maybe she had heard the story of Bartimaeus or the woman at the well. Maybe she was there that morning when the woman was caught in adultery or heard about the woman with the issue of blood.

In any event, she knew Jesus had the words of life. She didn't just understand forgiveness; she lived it. It was her story of undeserved, extravagant grace. She wasn't forgiven much because she loved much. But rather, she was able to love much because she was forgiven much.

She understood the meaning of Jesus's costly death on the cross, and she had made it her own. She knew she couldn't earn it and didn't deserve it. Now she was free, free to love Jesus with reckless passion and abandon.

Her love was extreme and lavish. There wasn't anything calculated or measured about it. She didn't blot his feet with perfume; she dumped the whole bottle. She was completely undone and overwhelmed by Jesus and his love for her. Love just poured out of her. She simply wanted to be with him.

She was free to risk humiliation and pain. She had gained the courage it took to come to Simon's house that night. The risk was well worth it. In her mind, nothing matched the surpassing value of knowing Christ and his love for her.

FULLY LOVED

David loves me a lot like God loves me, just as I am. He doesn't need me to pray better or think better or read my Bible more or even stop doing certain things. He loves me—flat out loves me despite all those things. He loves me more.

Just like I am David's dad and he loves me unconditionally, so am I God's son and he loves me outrageously, recklessly, and with undeserved goodness, power, and strength. Without limit or condition. No matter what, he loves first.

I also know, for Jesus, his love cost him. It is a costly grace. In *Romans* Paul says, "God demonstrates his own love for us in this: while we were still sinners, Christ died for us" (*Romans 5:8*). He loved us so much that he was willing to die for me and for you, to die for our sins, to die that we might know life—to suffer fully and completely so that we might know freedom and grace. This woman knew that.

"Jesus said to the woman, 'Your faith has saved you; go in peace.'"

JOURNAL

Think of a person that when you are around them you feel most loved, accepted, fully embraced, and able to be yourself. What about that person makes you feel that way?

_____

_____

_____

_____

_____

How did Jesus make this woman feel? Why do you think she came that night? Why do you think she loved Jesus so extravagantly, so recklessly?

_____

_____

_____

_____

_____

How does Jesus love you? Why does he love you? How can you best _live into_ that love?

_____

_____

_____

_____

_____

PRAY

Jesus, I thank you today that you love me with a reckless love. Thank you for the people in my life and the places that remind me of your love. You created me. You are crazy about me. There is nothing I can do to earn or deserve it. You just flat out "love me more." I am yours, and you are mine. Thank you, Jesus.

17

Surrender

"Sir," the woman said, "you have nothing to draw with and the well is deep. Where can you get this living water?" (John 4:11).

READ

Psalm 18
John 4:1-26

SILENCE.

When we used to drive a lot, David would ride in the back seat. We had a large minivan, and even when it was just the two of us, he would sit in the far back. He loved to be chauffeured. "Take it away, John," he would say.

He also absolutely knew the way home (from just about anywhere). He had it memorized. From almost five miles away he could tell you every turn: when to go right, when to go left, and what was coming next.

Every once in a while, Gae and I would need to stop on our way home at the grocery store or to get gas or to pick up one of the other kids. We would take a sharp right when he knew we should be taking a left.

"Where are you taking me!" he would yell from the back seat. Hilarious. As if we were kidnapping him.

"We aren't taking you anywhere. We are your parents. We need to get gas."

"Oh."

For David, it wasn't an issue of trust. It was more a point of information, but it sure sounded funny when he said it.

LET GO

One of the most difficult things in life is for us to give up—to let go. We are taught from the time we are babies to never quit, to hang in there, to stay in control, to never let the other get the upper hand, to not tap out, and to fight to the bitter end. Surrender is for quitters, and quitters are losers. Mostly.

Surrender is counterintuitive. Letting go, releasing, opening your hands, and allowing God feels like the least natural, and even least helpful, thing to do in almost every situation. Control, work harder, make it happen, and get 'er done—we've been taught these things since we were kids.

David doesn't have that gear. He lives open-handed. He waits. He watches. He listens. He trusts. He trusts me completely— for his food, his shelter, his education, his means of travel, his safety in getting there, his very life—and he's very much at peace with that.

CHORES

One of my all time favorite stories in scripture is in *John 4*. I think of this woman getting up that morning, thinking of all the chores she needed to get done—sweeping the house, cooking dinner, taking out the trash, going to the grocery store, doing the laundry, getting the kids off to school.

She also knew at some point she would need to get water. But she waited. Fetching water was a community event, a gathering place where you often saw friends and neighbors and other women and caught up on news and the latest gossip, the neighborhood chitchat.

She thought, "Maybe it is better to wait until later in the day when less people are there than to deal with the crowds early in the morning."

She had no idea who she would meet that day.

I wonder even as she walked there late that morning if she felt different—a certain lightness, an expectation—not even sure why or what, just that something felt very different. Something was about to change.

LIVING WATER

Jesus, tired from the journey, sat down by the well. And as he sits, this woman, a Samaritan, who had come to draw water, joins him.

"Can you draw me a drink, please?" asked Jesus.

The woman, somewhat taken aback by this, says, "You are a Jew and I am a Samaritan woman. How can you ask me for a drink?"

Jesus answers, "If you knew the gift of God and who it is that asks you for a drink, you would have asked him, and he would have given you living water."

She goes on, "Sir, you have nothing to draw with and the well is deep. Where can you get this living water?"

Then there is a sharp right hand turn.

Jesus answered, "Everyone who drinks from this water will thirst again, but whoever drinks from the water I give him, will never thirst, indeed the water I give him will become a spring of water welling up to eternal life."

I think of this woman and how she desperately tried to make her life work, how she landed her full trust, her self-worth, her sense of who she was and how others thought of her, her sense of identity and purpose, in a relationship with a man. Maybe at some level she recognized, even knew, that there was a gap, a hole, something not quite right, something empty. And she tried, desperately tried, over and over again to fill it.

And probably, for a time, it worked—until it didn't.

SURRENDER

And then she became miserable. Hoping to have someone fulfill in her something that only Jesus could, she became, as many of us do, *thirsty*—what was once shiny and new, what had brought her such *fun* and *happiness*, now became a source of frustration, irritation, aggravation, brokenness, and pain.

So she moved on—hoping and thinking, maybe not even consciously, certainly not out loud, that perhaps the next guy or the next thing would satisfy her. All the while trying to harness this deep ache inside, this yearning for wholeness, for real satisfaction, for water, but not just any water, real thirst-quenching water, water for the soul, something that she so desperately wanted— water that would spring up in her to eternal life.

She was exhausted.

And finally, she surrendered.

She comes and she sits down next to Jesus. He offers her what she has been looking for her whole life—the kind of water that is thirst quenching, that will spring up in her forever and forever, that will give her true life, joy, peace, meaning, belonging, identity—everything she has been looking for. And she gave in, she collapsed, she said yes and meant it. That day, as the Bible says, she became a new creation (*II Corinthians 5:17*).

EMBRACED

I think of this woman and there are times when I feel sorry for her. How hard of a life that must have been. How desperate. How *wishful*. How seemingly one failed relationship led to another and another.

And then I think, *How much different am I?* Deep, penetrating satisfaction, wholeness, grounded, embraced, beloved, a powerful identity—knowing that I am fully his. I understand all that, but do I believe it, really believe it? That it isn't what I do, what I accomplish, what I achieve, and it isn't what I produce that makes me who I am—it is who I am in Jesus, how he sees me—I am his *beloved*, rescued, won, pursued, bought back, redeemed, made whole, and a child, an actual son or daughter, of the King. It's not because of what I got done today or how great a leader I want to be or how many kids we are reaching or what someone said about me or how much money I make or the car I drive or the neighborhood I live in or even how well my kids are doing— all those are fleeting and temporary, they satisfy for a moment, maybe last for a time, but will always leave me thirsty.

Only Jesus offers us living water, water that will continue to spring up in us, that will continue to give us identity, purpose, strength, power, and meaning beyond who we are or what we do. We are his and he flat out loves us.

PARABLE

Jesus tells this parable in *Luke 6*, "Why do you call me Lord, Lord and do not do what I say? I will show you what he is like who hears my words and puts them into practice. He is like a man building a house, who dug down deep and laid the foundation on rock" (*v. 46-48*).

I am distracted and wooed by so many things. But my only real desire, my real heart's desire, is to find rock; deep rock, bedrock—to find it and build there. As Tim Keller likes to say, "If you give yourself to anything, anything other than Jesus—be it family, career, kids, money, status, power, or even knowledge or wisdom—it will eventually enslave you."

Only one thing, one thing, is meant to be worshipped, to be given our full attention—only one thing is able to give us real, thirst-quenching, living water that will continue to spring up in us to eternal life. And that one thing is Jesus.

And it begins with surrender.

JOURNAL

What do you wake up most mornings thinking about? What's the next big thing? What are you hoping to gain, achieve, accomplish, or get to that will satisfy that thirst in you?

_____

_____

_____

_____

_____

What was this woman looking for? Where was she hoping to find it? What did Jesus offer her? How was that different?

_____

_____

_____

_____

_____

What would surrender look like for you? What would it mean to leave some old things behind in order to find real, living water? How do you let go and put your full trust in Jesus?

_____

_____

_____

_____

_____

PRAY

I am hungry and thirsty, Jesus. I confess there is an ache in me that I have tried to fill with achievement, approval, other people, relationships, power, money, and things—and I am exhausted. I surrender. I give up and let go. I can't do it. I want real, deep, cold, thirst-quenching, living water—water that will spring up in me to eternal life. I am done looking. I am done searching. I give my heart, my trust, my life, and myself fully to you.

18

Slobberknocker

"Many tax collectors and sinners were eating with him and his disciples, for there were many who followed him" (Mark 2:15).

READ

Psalm 38
Mark 2:13-17

SILENCE.

This has been a brutal winter. Maybe a colder winter than I can ever remember. I think we have set records here in the city. I know they have in Boston.

David loves to go sledding. When it starts snowing, he can hardly contain himself. "Sledding, Daddy?" (Notice he doesn't say, "Sledding, Mommy?")

There are a few things David loves about sledding. First, speed—the faster the better. He wants to be flying. He wants the wind whipping against his face, eyes tearing up, the sled coming off the snow, and snot coming out the nose—just flying.

Then he wants danger. Trees, rocks, cliffs, other kids, dogs—if every run ended in us smashing the sled into a huge fence post or rock wall somewhere he would love it. He thinks that's hilarious.

If all that isn't enough, we get to the bottom, we are almost always together riding tandem, and the sled stops, and we roll off, get up, and walk back up the hill.

No, the sled stops and David rolls over on top of me, and it is a full on knockdown, drag-out *slobberknocker*. This is why mom doesn't get invited. We are wrestling, grunting, laughing, kicking, laughing, flipping, holding, grabbing, laughing, and sweating. It usually ends one of two ways: I either shake myself free, get up, and run for the top of the hill with the sled, or David wets his pants. Those are the only two ways it ends. People look at us like we are nuts.

I am way too old for this.

I think Jesus would love sledding with David.

TAX COLLECTOR

One of my favorite encounters in the Gospels is in *Mark 2*. Jesus is again walking beside the lake. A crowd follows him. Imagine that. Literally every time he walks out of the house, a group of people are waiting—so curious, so wanting and wondering, so hoping.

This day he sees Levi. Levi is a tax collector. He has made his living—a really good living—by collecting taxes from his fellow Jews and giving it to the hated Roman oppressors. Those who collected taxes were despised. Not only did they collect the tax for the Roman government, they often took more than they should and gave the Romans their share and pocketed the rest. They became very rich.

You can imagine as Jesus approaches Levi the murmuring that was going on with the disciples. "Hey, whoa, wait a minute—this guy! Oh no, I didn't sign up to hang out with this guy. A zealot maybe, a few fisherman, yes, but this clown? A tax collector? Are you kidding?"

SAW LEVI

Obviously when Jesus saw Levi he saw something different than maybe what Peter or James or John saw. He knew one day he would run upon another tax collector in a tree, a man named Zaccheus, and he would want to have lunch with Zaccheus. And maybe, just maybe, Zaccheus would look at this group following Jesus and think, "Wow, there's Levi. He seems to love Levi. Maybe it's ok. Maybe I can do this."

One thing I love about my son David is that he doesn't have the same categories for people that I do. People are just people. David doesn't separate the world into people who are like him and people who are different or rich and poor or Democrats and Republicans or black and white or Jews and Christians or even believers and non-believers. For David, people are people, and he simply loves them all. I think Jesus thinks a lot the same way.

And so Jesus looks at Levi and he says, "Come, follow me." And he does. That is amazing in and of itself. The Bible doesn't say what he does with the money that's laying there or his business or maybe people that are standing in line waiting for him. He simply gets up and follows Jesus.

HOUSE OF LEVI

And then the next part is even more amazing. It says that Jesus goes to Levi's house, and Levi has a party for him. The Bible says that the house was filled with tax collectors and sinners. It's a *slobberknocker*. Jesus is right there in the middle of it. The part I like the most is where it says, "For there were many who followed him." These weren't just Levi's friends. A lot of these were Jesus's friends.

And I have to think he loved being there.

It was rude and loud. My guess is there was some beer drinking and some foul language and some grunting, laughing, sweating, and maybe a dirty joke or two—these weren't choirboys. These guys rode Harley's and had tattoos and said the wrong things and didn't go to school and had nicknames like "Bones" and "Chub" and weren't the kids you hoped your kids were hanging out with. These were the "bad" kids.

RELENTLESS

One of the things that I have loved over the years about Young Life is how we relentlessly go after *sinners*. When I was a freshman in college at Wake Forest University in Winston-Salem, NC, I went to do what we call contact work with my area director, Fil Anderson. I loved Fil. I thought he was a good Christian and was excited to go with him to the high school.

We get out of the car in the parking lot and there are a group of guys standing over by one of the cars smoking cigarettes. All I can think is, *I hope we don't go over there and talk to those guys.*

Sure enough, Fil makes a beeline right to them. I am scared to death. He is standing there talking to this one kid and looks over and says, "Can I have a drag off your cigarette?" Fil takes the cigarette, pushes it up his nose, inhales, blows smoke out his mouth, takes the cigarette out of his nose, and hands it back to the kid.

The kid is looking at his cigarette, looking at Fil, looking at the cigarette. I thought, *That is the coolest thing I have ever seen.* I found two packs of cigarettes and went back to my dorm and started lighting them and sticking them up my nose and inhaling.

My roommate said, "What are you doing?"

And I said, "I am learning to be a Young Life leader."

NOT THE HEALTHY

The Pharisees and teachers of the law are watching all this through the window. Finally, they have had enough, and one of them turns to one of the disciples and says, "Why does he eat with sinners and tax collectors?"

I love this part. Jesus, knowing what they were thinking, says, "It is not the healthy who need a doctor but the sick. I have not come to call the righteous, but sinners."

I don't think Jesus was uncomfortable at Levi's house. I don't think he wondered why he was there or how he got there. He was there on purpose.

In *Luke 4*, Jesus is in the synagogue and he reads, "The Spirit of the Lord is on me, because he has anointed me to preach good news to the poor. He has sent me to proclaim freedom for the prisoners and recovery of sight for the blind, to release the oppressed, to proclaim the year of the Lord's favor" (*v. 18-19*).

Good news for the poor, freedom for prisoners, recovery of sight for the blind, and release for the oppressed. Over and over again we see him with prostitutes, thieves, felons, the unclean, lepers, the blind, the homeless, the disabled, the marginalized, the discarded, the invisible, the beat down, and the left out.

What happened at Levi's house that evening wasn't just something that happened. It was intentional. It was thought through. It was who Jesus was. It was his nature, his mission— "I have not come to call the righteous, but sinners." He literally couldn't help himself. He loved it. And it probably happened over and over again.

After every ride down the hill, David rolls over and looks at me with a big, silly grin on his face and says, "Again!"

And I say, "One more time, David."

And he says, "No, ten more times."

JOURNAL

What comes to mind when you think about spending time with *sinners*? When was the last time you were with a group of people like they had at Levi's house that evening? How did that feel?

Why do you think Jesus chose Levi to follow him? Why do you think he wanted to go to his house and have dinner? What was the Pharisees reaction to that?

Today, if Jesus walked the earth, whom do you think he would spend most of his time with? How does that sync up with how you spend your time? What does he mean when he says, "I have not come to call the righteous, but sinners?"

PRAY

Jesus, I confess that I am a sinner saved by grace. Thank you for how you love all people, me included. Give me the courage today to be in places and with people that might be hard for me, that might make me feel uncomfortable, with people that may look different or think different. These are places and people you love, people you died for and who break your heart. Thank you that you are already there; you are there with me. Help me to see with your eyes, feel with your heart, and touch with your hands.

19

Gratitude and the Power of Great

"When she heard about Jesus, she came up behind him in the crowd and touched his cloak" (Mark 5:27).

READ

Psalm 145
Mark 5:21-34

SILENCE.

I see David almost every morning, and every morning my first question is the same. "How was your nite-nite?"

"Great!" David says.

Not "good," not "okay," not "well, I slept well until about 2:30 then had to get up to go to the bathroom and had a hard time getting back to sleep," which is my typical response.

David has never met a bowl of spaghetti or a bowl of ice cream that he didn't think was great, or a swimming pool or a ride in the park or a trip to the toy store. Often he will look up and look at me and say, "Thank you, Daddy."

I know for a fact that not all of his "nite-nites" are great. He gets woken up by his brother or sister, a barking dog, a loud noise, we have to get him up early for school, or whatever it is, but that doesn't matter. His response is always, "Great." Not every bowl of spaghetti is served the way he likes it or every bowl of ice cream. That's okay with David. He says, "It's great, thank you, Daddy."

MORE

In general, I think that is not the world we live in. The world we live in teaches us to be critical, to not be satisfied, to always want or expect something more, to live in this perpetual state of "if only." If only she had gotten here sooner. If only I didn't have to wait for him. If only we made a little more money, had a bigger house, and a bigger yard. If only my kids had gotten into that school or we lived in that neighborhood or my parents were a bit more supportive or I got that promotion I was hoping for or I was a few inches taller or a few pounds lighter—we simply live in a solid state of, "I wish my life were different." For the most part, we are simply ungrateful.

Gratitude is a learned skill in my opinion. You have to practice it. For most of us, it just doesn't come naturally. I think it is linked closely to humility, which is why David is so good at it. For some reason, I think I deserve better. He never does.

A CERTAIN WOMAN

When I think of gratitude, I often think of this woman. For twelve years she suffered. She went to doctor after doctor, appointment after appointment. How hard would it have been to continue to go back to the doctor, knowing that you were spending all the money you had and were not only not getting better, you were getting worse?

GAE CALLED

Just a little over two years ago now, I was sitting in the office when Gae called, which honestly she rarely does in the middle of the day. As soon as I answered I could tell something was wrong.

"I need you to come home," she said.

"What's wrong?" I answered. I could hear the tears.

"I just need you to come home."

"What is it?"

"I have cancer."

I hung up the phone and curled over in my chair. It was like taking a punch to the gut. The air was knocked out of me. What did she say? What? Cancer? Gae had had a mammogram several weeks prior. The doctor had said she wanted to run a few more tests. She had a biopsy. But all the while, Gae was very upbeat and had at least given me the impression this was fairly routine, that women go through this and most tests come back negative and she just wants to be sure.

HOLDING ON

I was on a conference call but quickly excused myself, gathered my stuff, and headed for the subway. I was dazed, in shock. Tears were streaming down my cheeks. I was being pushed and jostled by the crowd. I kept moving if for no other reason than to keep from falling. I went down the steps and into the subway. I finally made it to the front door of our apartment. Jessi was home. We sat on the bed. We held each other. And we cried.

What now? What next? What are you thinking, God?

Gae had an operation in mid-June, then eight treatments of chemo over sixteen weeks, then five weeks of radiation. We weren't fully done until January.

The hardest part is holding on to hope over the course of eight months. It is easy to focus on what isn't right or what isn't good. David was amazing. All he really knew was "Mommy doesn't feel good." There were good days and bad days. Lots of days my only job was to get David out of the house and "go do something." So there were plenty of long bike rides in the park and trips to the playground and a short walk to get ice cream.

God was gracious. I tried to be grateful. Gae was amazing. It seemed that at the most desperate moments, when I literally thought I couldn't take another step, Jesus would show up and give me the strength to go just a little further.

ONE DAY

That's where this woman was, desperate and holding on. And one day, Jesus showed up. It is hard to know what she knew about Jesus before that day. But we do know, if Mark has written at all chronologically, that the leper had been healed in *Mark 1*, that prior to that happening the whole town had gathered at the door in Capernaum, and he had healed all of their diseases. He had healed the paralytic in *Mark 2*, calmed the storm in *Mark 4*, and at the beginning of this chapter he had cast demons out of the man called Legion.

News spread fast in those days, so much so that before Jesus could even land the boat at the beginning of this story "a large crowd" had gathered. This woman, at the very least, knew Jesus had the power to heal and do so dramatically. She came with a holy expectation. And she wasn't going to be denied.

"If I just touch his clothes, I will be healed," she says in *verse 28*. She pushes through the crowd. She is getting closer—being pushed and shoved. She finally gets there, reaches out her hand, and "touches his cloak," and the Bible says, "Immediately her bleeding stopped and she felt in her body that she was freed from her suffering" (*v. 29*).

DEEPLY GRATEFUL

Do you think she was grateful? Do you think after that she ever complained about not having the right shoes to wear to church or not being able to find a parking space or about someone showing up late to a meeting or the elevator not working in her building or not being able to access the Food Channel or her spaghetti not being exactly the way she likes it?

Tim Keller likes to say, "If we truly understood the truth of the gospel, truly got it, truly understood what Jesus has done for us, got it down deep in the depth of our souls, we would be a much more grateful people." We are all this woman. We are dead in our sin. We are trying desperately to fill our miserable lives. We are trying repeatedly to stuff something into our hearts that will ease the pain. Trying anything, even if it hurts, that might numb it, even for a few hours.

As a teenager I did that by having a few beers with my friends or washing my car or going out with my girlfriend or having a good game. As an adult it has turned into being successful in my job or buying that house in the right neighborhood or having my kid get into the right school or thinking about the next vacation. It all amounts to about the same thing: temporary relief from an aching pain.

What this woman understood was that only Jesus can provide real relief, real freedom, and real meaning, purpose, and healing. Only Jesus can truly satisfy our deepest hurt, our greatest thirst, and our deepest need. Jesus and Jesus alone. Everything else is temporary, at best.

And when we touch even the hem of his garment and we realize that we have been made whole, that our bleeding has stopped, that we have truly been set free, we begin to become grateful people.

WHOLE STORY

In the middle of this crowd, with people pushing and jostling against him, Jesus stopped and said, "Who touched me?"

"The woman knowing what had happened to her, came and fell at his feet" (v. 33).

The very next line says, "And she told him her whole story." Can you imagine? What dignity and importance he showed this woman. With this huge crowd around him, Jairus, a very influential leader waiting for him, and the disciples getting impatient, Jesus sits down, and he listens. He elevates her just by his attention. He looks at her as she is talking.

"You are well," he says. "All of you."

I love the fact that in the mission of Young Life, we often stop long enough to listen to a kid's story, to their whole story. I think of the many people who have stopped long enough to hear my story. And I am deeply grateful for how when Gae was sick, there were a few people who listened to my story almost daily.

GO IN PEACE

Jesus said as she walked away, "Daughter, your faith has healed you. Go in peace and be freed from your suffering."

I can only imagine that after that day when she would wake in the morning and one of her kids would say, "Hey, Mom, how was your nite-nite?"

She would look back, smile, and say, "It was great! Really great!"

JOURNAL

Think about a time when you were desperate, when you had tried just about everything, and rather than getting better, you had gotten worse.

_____

_____

_____

_____

_____

What difference did it make for this woman that Jesus showed up that day? How about the fact that he stopped, that he saw her and he listened to her whole story? Where has Jesus shown up for you? Is he willing to stop? Is he willing to listen?

_____

_____

_____

_____

What is your deepest source of gratitude? How does life change when you wake up every day alive and grateful?

_____

_____

_____

_____

PRAY

Jesus, we start and end this day grateful, grateful that your powerful touch has healed us and made us whole. We no longer live as desperate people, even in the face of hurt, brokenness, and pain. We are grateful for your touch that frees us and relieves our suffering. Thank you that you stop and wait and listen. You listen and hear our whole story. Thank you, Jesus.

20

Courage

"Jesus, Son of David, have mercy on me!" (Mark 10:47).

READ

Psalm 16
Mark 10:46-52

SILENCE.

A couple of months ago, David's school had their fall dance. One of the things Gae and I love about this school is that although it is a school primarily for kids with special needs, they do everything a typical high school would do—they have dances and a prom, they have a school musical and a basketball team, they have a yearbook club and a cooking club, they decorate for Halloween and Valentine's Day, they have something almost every week that says, "You are in high school and we want you to do high school things."

David had never been to a dance. He loves to dance but at home, in the mirror or with his sister or in his underwear. He'd never been to a dance, and he'd certainly never been to a dance where there were girls—"Uggggh, I hate girls!"

ZOEY

David also has a crush on Zoey. Zoey is a cute-as-a-button little girl in David's class who has Down syndrome that he talks about constantly. On "Twin Day," Zoey's mom sent an outfit home with David with a note that said, "Zoey would like to be "twins" with David tomorrow. Is it okay if he wears this outfit?" Hilarious. Obviously Zoey had been talking a little about David as well.

Apparently, Zoey was going to be at the dance. High school is so hard. I hated stuff like this. On the one hand you want to go, you want to see that one cute girl who you think, you hope, likes you. And, on the other hand, you are scared out of your mind. You break into a sweat just thinking about it.

As a guy it was always easier to go outside and play ball and try to hurt each other or go over to someone's house and read comic books and talk about girls. I guess today guys play video games so that they don't have to talk to anyone, which is probably even better.

THE DANCE

David wanted to go to the dance. We had talked about it all week. You could just tell he was scared to death. Who would be there? What would it be like? Would the music be loud? Would it be dark? Would there be kissing? I guess Gae and I wondered the same thing, about the kissing part that is.

One thing we had decided is that we wouldn't be there. We would drop him off and leave. The last thing you want as a high school kid is to have your parents at the high school dance—I don't care who you are. There can't be a bigger loser moment than a kid looking over your shoulder and saying, "Hey, dude, is that your mom?" We weren't going to let that happen to David.

So the plan was to get him to the door, get him in the hands of a responsible adult, and then hit it. We had some friends in town so that made it easier. We would drop David off at the dance, go to dinner somewhere close (especially if it didn't go well and they needed us for some reason), and then come back in a couple of hours and pick him up.

IN THE DOOR

Well, as we had figured, we got maybe twenty feet from the door of the school and David plops down on the sidewalk. "No, don't go. Dance all done. Go home." Gae and I weren't surprised. This is often part of the drill with David.

Tons of kids and parents are stepping over him to get in the door. "Look, David, there's Sam. There's Alex. There's Richard." Wow, if Zoey were there and could come out and ask David to come in. Man alive. Game over. Just like in most of my high school career—it didn't happen.

Finally, with a bit of coaxing and some help from our friends and a couple of teachers, we got David in the door. We saw Ms. Clancy and Mr. Tabone. They both came over and said hello to David, gave us the thumbs up, and we were out the door. When we left, David was in the hallway, sitting on the floor.

BARTIMAEUS

One of my favorite characters in the Bible is Bartimaeus. Bartimaeus is blind and he is a beggar. He is hungry and alone. He is at the mercy of those who pass by. Days are long and lonely. Life for the most part is tough. Some days he gets enough for bread and a bit to drink, but most days, not much.

Bartimaeus, maybe blind from birth, had anything but a normal life. He had never held a job. He had probably never gone to school, had few friends, had little he could do to pass the time, and had never seen a sunset or the ocean or maybe been to a birthday party. He had little in the way of family or support and had certainly never been to the high school dance.

So each day he gathered his stuff, walked out to the street between Jericho and Jerusalem, plopped down, and began begging. Everyone knew him. People saw him every day. It was Bartimaeus and he was a beggar.

A BUZZ

Except for this day. This day would be different. There was a bit of a buzz in the air. Something was happening and Bartimaeus could feel it. He wasn't sure if there was a show in town or a festival of sorts or a band was playing—but something was happening and it was exciting.

Bartimaeus could hear the crowd—people talking, laughing. But they were still a far way off. As they got closer he realized it was more than a crowd. There was something happening here. He asked a friend, "What's going on? What's all the fuss about?"

He had heard of this guy Jesus of Nazareth. But he wasn't sure who he was. Some said he was a teacher. Others said he was a healer—a miracle worker of sorts. A few others had actually said, "He's the Son of God, the Messiah."

And then his buddy said, "You haven't heard? It's Jesus, Jesus of Nazareth, with his disciples. Heading to Jerusalem."

JESUS OF NAZARETH

"What? Are you kidding me? Jesus? Jesus of Nazareth coming down my street? Today?" The crowd got louder. I could hear people talking. I thought, "This could be my chance. I may never have a chance like this again."

And so I shouted, "Jesus, Son of David, have mercy on me!"

People in the crowd began to yell back. "Shut up! Be quiet you beggar! Keep it down over there! He doesn't want to speak to you!" they shouted.

It would have been easy to quit.

I thought, "No, this is my shot. I may never have this chance again. This may be as close as I ever get to Jesus."

"Jesus, Son of David, have mercy on me!" I shouted again.

I felt him stop.

CALL HIM HERE

"Call him here," Jesus said.

Wow, he's calling for me. People in the crowd started saying, "Hey, he's calling for you."

I jumped up and without thinking threw my cloak and began to run to him. Knocking into people. Fumbling through the crowd, finally I made it to Jesus.

I felt his warm eyes look at me. "What is it you want me to do for you?"

"I want to receive my sight. I want to see, Jesus. I want to be like my friends. I want to be whole. I want to see."

"Go," said Jesus. "Your faith has healed you."

"Immediately," the Bible says, "he received his sight and followed Jesus along the road." Dancing.

THE DANCE

When Gae and I got back to the dance that night, one of the teachers grabbed us and said, "You have to come see this." We looked in the auditorium and all the kids were dancing in this huge congo line. Up front leading the way, was our son David, arms over his head and a huge grin on his face. Dancing up a storm. Looking over his shoulder at the line. Hilarious. What great courage. What a leader. What a gift.

JOURNAL

Think of a time when you exercised great courage? How did it feel? Why were you afraid? What were others around you saying?

_____

_____

_____

_____

_____

Why would this have been hard for Bartimaeus? What did he overcome? Why did Jesus stop? Would he have stopped for you?

_____

_____

_____

_____

_____

If Jesus were to ask you, "What do you want me to do for you?" how would you answer him? What would the crowd and those close say to you?

_____

_____

_____

_____

_____

PRAY

Dear Jesus, thank you for your courage. Thank you that you hear me. Thank you that you are willing to stop. Thank you that when I am unwilling to cry out, you cry out for me. Thank you, Jesus, that when the crowd tells me to be quiet, you encourage me to speak. Thank you that you have the power to make me whole, to heal—body, mind, and soul. I give you this day. Help me to live courageously today. Help me to dance.

21

Good Game

"Early in the morning, Jesus stood on the shore,
but the disciples did not realize that it was Jesus" (John 21:4).

READ

Psalm 147
John 21:1-14

SILENCE.

David loves baseball. So do I. Every chance we get, I grab a bat and a ball and we hit a few. We work on his stance, balance, foot work, hands, and swing. He loves it.

Previously, we had been a part of a league in the DC area that was all kids with disabilities. The "buddies" were kids from the Georgetown Prep baseball team. They were great with David and he loved being with them.

When we arrived in New York, we looked for something similar but couldn't find it. Finally, Gae happened upon a league on the Upper West Side that was very similar to what we remembered in DC.

David loved it, once we actually got him on the field that is. Typically a game is only a couple of innings and each inning every kid gets a chance to bat, no matter how many outs there are. Each kid also keeps swinging until they actually hit the ball.

When David first started playing, no matter where or how hard he hit the ball, he would run all the way around the bases. When he got to home he would slow down a bit, jump on the plate, throw his hands up in the air, and yell, "Home run."

We would all cheer, "Home run, David! Way to go!" Then he would run around slapping everyone high fives.

GOOD GAME

One of his favorite parts of the game was at the end, when the coach would pull all the kids together and they would put their hands in the middle and he would say, "On the count of three yell, 'Go Astros!'"

Then the kids would all line up and walk alongside the players from the other team, slap high fives, and say, "Good game, good game, good game."

So one day, after the game, we were doing this and I noticed instead of "good game," one kid is saying, "I hate Justin Bieber. I hate Justin Bieber. I hate Justin Bieber."

I thought, *Okay, that's funny.*

David and I do it more the traditional way. We simply say, "Good game, good game." Then pack up and get on our tandem bike and start riding home. Of course David still has on his uniform. As we ride through the streets David looks at the people on the sidewalks and says, "Good game, good game."

They are unsure of what to say in return. "Oh, thanks," or, "You too," or, "Good game."

We get to the intersection of 84th and Broadway and the light turns red, so we stop. There must be a hundred people crossing the street. David is saying "good game, good game" to each one of them.

Some look annoyed. Others nod. Some say, "Good game." I've pretty much lost control of myself at that point.

LIVING LIFE

Living life with David you just can't take yourself too seriously. You often find yourself engaging total strangers—people on the bus, in the grocery store, on an airplane, in the men's room, on the elevator—people you would otherwise have nothing in common with and would never speak to. But, for some reason, David just walks up to them and says, "Howdy partner," or "Aye, aye, Captain," or gives them a big hug or tries to swing them like you are square dancing. So there you are, saying hello to your new friend.

Living life with Jesus had to be like that, unpredictable; you were never sure what might happen next, even after Jesus has been crucified and laid in a tomb, things could get crazy in a hurry.

GOING FISHING

One of my favorite stories is in *John 21*.

In *John 20*, just a chapter before, Peter and John ran to the empty tomb, raced actually, and were stunned when Jesus wasn't there. They run back home. Then there are two angels dressed in white. Jesus appears to Mary there in the garden, then to the twelve disciples and to Thomas. But for some reason, you turn the page and they are going fishing, almost like nothing happened, like nothing ever, like we are going back to where we started, to the very beginning, to what we know.

Peter looks at the crew in *v. 3* of chapter 21 and says, "I'm going fishing."

James and Andrew both say, "Me too." And off they go.

They fish all night, as was their custom. And in the morning they haven't caught a thing (story of my life). So they start rowing in. And there is Jesus on the shore. And it says, "But they didn't recognize him." Really? They didn't recognize Jesus? Did he have on a hat and a pair of nose glasses? My guess is he had been up most the night thinking about this prank.

"Hey, fellas, did you catch anything?" I love that. He knows they didn't catch anything. This is Jesus we're talking about.

"No," they answered. You can just see him snickering at this point.

RIGHT SIDE

"Throw your nets over the right side of the boat and you will find some." This is going to be awesome, he thought.

"Oh, the right side of the boat. Hadn't thought of that. Been out here all night and just been fishing off the left side."

The crazy thing is they do it. They still don't recognize that it's Jesus, but rather than ask a lot of questions, they just fire the nets over the right side of the boat. And now, for the first time all night, maybe the first time in a really long time, they can't haul them in. Their nets are bursting with fish.

"I know who this is," says Peter.

A big grin comes up on Jesus's face. "Gotcha."

Peter dives in the water and runs up on shore. Jesus starts running, laughing. Peter chases Jesus down the beach. They are both laughing. He finally catches him and gets Jesus in a headlock and starts giving him a big nuggie. Jesus is crying laughing.

The other disciples finally get there and they dog pile on Jesus, wrestling, laughing.

"Did you catch anything?" Jesus says, and they all start laughing, belly laughing.

John says, "I knew it was you. I kept trying to tell them."

"Oh yea, you knew." And they just howl laughing.

BACON, EGGS, AND FISH

Jesus fixes breakfast. I love that. I love fixing pancakes and bacon on Saturday morning. We do it every week. David can sit down and eat five pancakes without blinking.

Jesus starts a fire, cooks up some of the fish, fries an egg or two, cooks some bacon, toasts some bread, brews some hot coffee, and it's just like old times—telling stories, laughing, eating, jokes, loving. The sun's hot, coffee's good, fire crackles, water is calm, and there's a slight breeze. It's beautiful. "Can you pass the bacon?"

Jesus looks at Peter, "Good game." They smile. A fish jumps. What a day.

JOURNAL

What makes you laugh? When was the last time you just belly laughed, doubled over, uncontrollable, lost it, tears even?

_____

_____

_____

_____

_____

Does Jesus have a sense of humor? How do you see it in this story? How does he engage the disciples? What event in the Gospels would you see Jesus laughing?

_____

_____

_____

_____

_____

Is life with Jesus fun, unpredictable? Does he cause you to laugh? When was the last time you found yourself in a situation with Jesus and thought, "Okay, this is hilarious"?

_____

_____

_____

_____

_____

PRAY

Thank you for the humor of life. Thank you that you go through large parts of your day with a smile on your face. Thank you that laughter is good for the heart, for the soul—that you love us, you created us, you live in us, and you also place us in crazy places and situations and with people who just make us laugh. And you laugh with us. And it is good.

22

Fear

"God did not give us a spirit of fear, but a spirit of power and of love and of self-discipline" (II Timothy 1:7).

READ

Psalm 40
Matthew 14:22-32

SILENCE.

David is afraid of a lot of things. He is afraid of little babies, especially when they are crying. He is afraid of barking dogs. He is afraid of any really loud noise. He is afraid of crowds. He is afraid of a room of strangers. Sometimes he is afraid of a room of family and friends.

Some of his fears seem rational and make *sense*. Others make no sense. When he was young and was afraid, he would lie down on the floor and, as Gae would like to say, "go boneless." There was little you could do to pick him up or move him at that point. The best you could do would be to literally *drag* him out of the way.

THE DOCTOR

Another fear David has is of any kind of doctor or exam. Not sure where Gae was this day, but somehow I drew the short straw and had to take him to the eye doctor. David was probably ten at the time, not a little boy.

He did fairly well waiting in the waiting room, playing with toys and looking at books, and finally his name was called. Miraculously, I was able to get him back to the examining room.

The woman who was to examine him was older, proper, in a dress, and not really sure what to think of David. David can smell fear or, at the very least, lack of confidence. This woman wore it like a suit.

HOLD HIM

At first, we had David sit up in the chair as she tried to examine him. She asked him a few questions, and then said, "I just need to have a peek into your eyes." David was having none of it.

Finally she said to me, "Why don't you sit with him on the floor and hold him." So he and I got on the floor, I somehow got behind him, the woman crouched down in front of him, and at the appropriate time I wrapped my arms around him and tried to hold him while the doctor attempted to look into his eyes.

Well David is strong, and he started pushing back, and the woman was then on the floor with us trying to get a peek into his eyes, and somehow in all the fray, she lost her balance and fell on top of us, and the three of us were rolling around on the floor together, and she still had her eye-checker thingie up to her eye trying to look in David's eyes, and I was sweating, and David was pushing harder, and I was trying to hold him still, and he was shouting, "All done, all done," and I could only think, *Is there training for this sort of thing? Maybe some kind of class or course I could take?*

REAL FEARS

So what about real fears? What about life-altering fears? What about things that literally keep us awake at night? Where do we find courage? Where do we place our trust, really?

In *Matthew 14*, Jesus has just experienced the trauma of hearing that his friend and cousin John the Baptist has been beheaded. Upon hearing the news, Jesus withdraws to a solitary place where he just happens to meet five thousand people—five thousand hungry people.

After providing bread and fish for the masses, he dismisses the crowd, and then the Bible says, "He made the disciples get into the boat."

I love that. Can't you just hear Peter saying, "You know, I don't think this is such a great idea."

And Jesus saying, "I'm not asking you to think. Get in the boat."

We've all been there. He needs some alone time. He gets the disciples in the boat and heads up the mountainside.

TAKE COURAGE! IT IS I! DON'T BE AFRAID.

Then the most bizarre thing happens. They are out in the boat, it is dark, and it is the fourth watch of the night, just before dawn, so maybe around 5 a.m. They have to be tired at this point, tired and scared. A storm is raging and Jesus comes walking to them out on the water. What? Graham Cooke says, "Jesus is consistent, but totally unpredictable." Walking on the water? Part of me thinks that when he decided to do that, a little grin came over his face. And they think he's a ghost.

Jesus says to the guys in the boat, "Take courage it is I. Don't be afraid."

And Peter replies, "Lord, if it is you, tell me to come to you on the water." What? Come to you on the water? Are you kidding? In the middle of a raging storm, at night, in the dark, in deep water, miles from shore, with no light and no lifejacket? He steps out of that boat, he's a goner.

So why, why in heaven's name, would Peter even begin to think about doing that? In the boat you have security, you have people, you have protection, you have comfort, you have control. What else would you want?

In the water you have danger, darkness, wind, waves, risk, and death. Why in the world would anyone get out of the boat?

Two reasons. In the water, you have Jesus—plain and simple. That's where he is. He's not in the boat. And secondly, he unmistakably called you to come out there. Period. No other reason. Apart from that, you best stay in the boat.

Listen to the words of Isaiah: "But now, this is what the Lord says, He who created you, O Jacob, he who formed you, O Israel. 'Fear not, for I have redeemed you; I have summoned you by name; you are mine, When you pass through the waters, I will be with you; and when you pass through the rivers, they will not sweep over you. When you walk through the fire, you will not be burned; the flames will not set you ablaze. For I am the Lord, your God, the Holy One of Israel, your Savior, I give

Egypt for your ransom, Cush and Seba in your stead. Since you are precious and honored in my sight, and because I love you'" (*Isaiah 43:1-4*).

"Take courage! It is I! Don't be afraid." This is who the Lord is and why he can say to us, "Don't be afraid." This is the one who calls you, who knows you, who created you and loves you, and he is begging you, "Don't be afraid. I am with you."

So when your wife calls you and says, "You need to come home. I have breast cancer," or one of the administrators from your child's school says, "You need to get up here. Your daughter is having a medical emergency," or the doctor turns around after examining your little boy and says, "I think he has Down syndrome," it is too late to start thinking about this.

You either believe it or you don't. You either practice it or you don't. God is either good or he isn't. He is either for you or he's not. You have either chosen to build your house on a rock or you haven't. You will either stand firm and let nothing move you or you will be wrecked.

HE WILL BE WITH US

Listen to what Jesus says:

He says, "I will be with you, I will never leave you or forsake you, I will stand in the midst of the storm and say to you, 'Take courage, it is I, it is Jesus, the God of the Universe, the Great I am, the one that even these winds and waves obey.'"

He says, "I will be your rock and your refuge, I will be your rest, your hiding place, in me and me alone can you trust."

He says, "I am the resurrection and the life, apart from me you can do absolutely nothing."

He says, "I created all things, they were created for me and by me and in me all things hold together."

He says, "I have not given you a spirit of fear, but a spirit of power and of love and of self discipline."

He says, "Above all else, I am good, I am consistent, I am honorable, I am powerful, I am committed, faithful and unchangeable. I am the Covenant Maker and the Covenant Keeper."

Your only real security is in the God who made you.

And then, when we have lost all confidence, when we have

done everything we can know to do to fix it, when we have exhausted all of our resources, wit, and education, when we have consulted every expert and specialist and still come to the end of our rope, and when we are rolling around on the floor with our son who is screaming his head off in fear, Jesus comes to us and says: "I have summoned you by name; you are mine. When you pass through the waters, I will be with you; and when you pass through the rivers, they will not sweep over you. When you walk through the fire, you will not be burned; the flames will not set you ablaze. For I am the Lord, your God, the Holy One of Israel, your Savior. I give Egypt for your ransom, Cush and Seba in your stead. Since you are precious and honored in my sight, and because I love you."

JOURNAL

What are you afraid of? Are you afraid of heights, the dark, bats, water, or people? What event or circumstance, if it happened, would you say, "I can't handle that"?

_____

_____

_____

_____

_____

How does Jesus enter into our fears? How does he stand with us and beside us? How does he give us courage?

_____

_____

_____

_____

_____

What in your life and my life will have the last word? Ultimately, in what will you put your trust?

_____

_____

_____

_____

_____

PRAY

Jesus, I will decide today that I will stand on this fact, that no matter what comes my way, no matter how hard or difficult or treacherous the storm, no matter how dark or unbearable it feels, that you will have the last word here over me, over my children, over my spouse, over our home, over my job. You will have the last word, Jesus, and I trust in you. I trust in you and you alone, you fully, all of your promises and nothing else. And if you call me out of the boat, I will come. I will get up. I will step out. I will move and I will not be afraid.

23

Give It a Shot

"Simon answered, 'Master, we've worked hard all night and haven't caught anything'" (Luke 5:5).

READ

Psalm 33
Luke 5:1-11

SILENCE.

David is a daredevil. He loves things that are fast and scary—in fact, the faster the better. But getting him to try something the first time is often a challenge. When he was young, we would sit at the bottom of the zip line at camp and watch the kids come down. I could tell David wanted to do it but just didn't have the courage to walk up that hill.

As Gae says, "baby steps." It won't all happen at once. So we would practice putting on a harness, splashing in the water, walking towards the top, looking at the tower where we clip in and jump off.

Finally, one day, David looks at me and says, "I'll give it a shot." He is so awesome. Takes him a while, you have to be patient, take small steps, but eventually, he's ready.

We get our harnesses and head for the top. I can tell he's nervous. So am I. But he's ready. We have momentum. We don't want to turn back now.

COUNT OF THREE

The summer-staff woman at the top is extra kind. David flirts with her. She flirts back. She checks our straps, pulls the carabineer, and we clip in and are ready to go. The lake looks a mile away. Nothing but wire, trees, rocks, and water between here and there.

I want to be sure David goes. I say, "On the count of three, one, two, three!!!"—I go on four. We step off the platform, and David's face just lights up. His eyes are as big as saucers. Within seconds we are flying—literally. The wire is buzzing; the wind is whipping through our hair. We pick up speed. He starts to yell. We both start yelling, "Hooooowheeeee!!!!" We finally break the tree line and are out over the lake. Kids are watching. We raise our legs and pull up on the rope to get a bit more distance and *whoosh*—we splash down in the water.

No sooner has David come to a stop when he looks over at me and says, "Again." Hilarious. The boy loves this stuff.

BY THE LAKE

One of my favorite stories in scripture is in *Luke 5* where we see Jesus once again walking beside the lake. It starts, "One day as Jesus was standing by the Lake of Gennesaret (or the Sea of Galilee) with the people crowding around him . . ." (*v. 1*). It is amazing how every time he left the house there was a crowd—people simply wanting to hear, to be with, to wait, to listen, to see.

And it says that there were two boats there—one happened to be Peter's. Jesus is no dummy. He is nothing if he isn't strategic. I think of how we are taught in Young Life to do "contact work"—as we go to a playground or to the school, you identify that kid you would like to meet, and you find a way to be hanging around his locker when he shows up or out at practice or somewhere you know you will casually bump into him. That was Jesus.

DEEP WATER

When he is finished speaking, he says to Peter, "Put out into the deep water and let down the nets for a catch." One thing that has become very evident to me over the years is that to follow Jesus often means you find yourself in deep water. Deep water can be scary. It can be dark. It involves a certain amount of risk and danger. There are often big creatures in deep water.

I love Peter's response. He is clear that this hasn't been a particularly easy night. He says, "Master, we've worked hard all night and haven't caught anything."

I think of how hard that work is: it is hot; the nets are heavy;

they have to throw them over and over again and each time haul them in; the boats are crude; they have to row; they work all night; they are exhausted; they haven't caught a thing; the sun is up; it is time to rest. Not to mention, there is a whole crowd of people now on the side of the lake thinking, "I've got to see this."

And here is one of my favorite responses of anyone in the Bible. Peter says, "But because you say so . . ." You know it doesn't make sense. They've been fishing all night. They have fished in deep water and shallow water, the back of the boat and the front of the boat, the right side and the left side. They are fisherman. They are exhausted. They are cleaning their nets. They are ready to go home.

635 L STREET

When I first came on Young Life staff, I moved into a small row house in DC at 635 L Street NE with two friends, Steve Hase and Scott Oostdyk. Behind our house was a playground that every evening would fill up with kids: riding bikes, jumping double-dutch, playing basketball—the music was blaring, it was hot, crowded, loud, you could smell the pavement and taste the popcorn. I would sit in our living room scared to death. I was tortured by thoughts like: *I ought to go out there. They will eat me alive. That's why I'm here. You're out of your mind. I will do it today. I promise.*

Nothing about it seemed to make sense. That's the point. It doesn't have to make sense when God tells you to do something. "But because you say so." I think of Moses going to Pharaoh or Samuel choosing David or Abraham sacrificing Isaac or Nehemiah rebuilding the wall or Sarah being pregnant or Noah building an ark or Peter getting out of the boat or Mary looking into the empty tomb or Paul going to Athens—it doesn't have to make sense that is the whole point.

LARGE NUMBER OF FISH

"When they had done so, they caught such a large number of fish that their nets began to break." It says, "They filled both boats so full they began to sink." That is a lot of fish. These are some big boats, enough to accomodate at least thirteen guys later in the Gospels. And they begin to sink!

Peter, seeing God's abundance, falls on his knees in the midst of this catch of fish and says, "Go away from me, Lord, I am a sinful man." We catch a glimpse, in the midst of this amazing miracle, of his deep brokenness and humility.

I think it is here, in the midst of literally a boatload of stinky fish, that Jesus realizes *this is my guy.*

"Don't be afraid," Jesus said. "From now on you will be fishing for men and women. So they pulled their boats up on shore, left everything, and followed Jesus" (*v. 10-11*).

I am not sure what the Greek is here for left everything, but I think it means that they "left everything"—family, friends, security, jobs, a couple big boat loads of fish, mom, dad, girlfriends, coffee makers, flat screens, porch swings, garage door openers. They left it all to follow Jesus.

They stand up on that platform, harnessed in, and Jesus says, "On the count of three." They step off together, their faces light up, their eyes are as big as saucers, and they are flying—literally. The wire is buzzing. The wind is whipping through their hair. They are picking up speed—and they all begin to yell, "Hooooowheeeee!"

JOURNAL

Looking back on your life, are there places and times when Jesus called you to something that just didn't make sense? What was your response?

_____

_____

_____

_____

_____

How does Jesus challenge the disciples in this story? What do you think were some of the responses running through Peter's mind? What allowed him to trust Jesus the way he did?

_____

_____

_____

_____

_____

Where do you see Jesus asking you to trust him now, maybe in ways that don't make sense? What could he be asking you to do or to consider in the future?

_____

_____

_____

_____

_____

PRAY

Dear Jesus, thank you for those times and places that you call us into "deep water." Let me have the kind of trust, the kind of willing faith that allowed Peter to say, "But because you say so." Everything else may not add up. Logically, it just doesn't make sense. But because you say so, I will go, and I will go with boldness.

24

Persistence

"Yet because of his persistence he will get up and give him as much as he needs" (Luke 11:8).

READ

Psalm 30
Luke 11:5-13

SILENCE.

One of the greatest lessons I think David has taught me over the years is the power of persistence. When we first moved to New York, we started going to All Angels Church on the Upper West Side. David doesn't do well with transition, and he doesn't do well with new places, especially new places that are filled with lots of people he doesn't know.

So the first few weeks, we didn't get near the door. If you are the person in Sam Shoemaker's "I Stand at the Door" you didn't see David because we didn't make it that far.

David would get to the corner of 80th and Broadway, which is maybe one hundred fifty yards from the church, and plop down on the sidewalk. And there he sat—immovable. You really couldn't reason with him or tell him it's going to be fine or just come check it out or these are nice people. None of that mattered to David.

So you waited. Waited until he was ready to get up and go. Typically either Gae or I would sit out with him, the other would go in, and then around "halftime" we would switch.

CLOSER

Each week David would get a few feet closer. This went on for eight months. Eight. Gae and I sitting out on the front steps watching and waiting on David while the other one is in the service. We met a lot of people.

Finally it started getting cold outside and we would say, "David, if you want to get warm, you are going to have to go inside." He didn't move.

And then, one Sunday, he did. It was like a miracle—a mid-February miracle. He just got up and walked through the front door of the church. I was stunned. He didn't say much, just walked in. First time I was truly grateful for really cold weather.

We got him upstairs to the gym, which was great, but then he was stuck again. He hung out in the gym for the better part of the next year or so—playing games, reading books, and watching his iPad. And then, by the grace of God, our friend Paul, who had been helping pretty much all along, was able to get David into the service.

So now we have five or six great friends who take turns being with him during the first part of the service, and then they bring him down and he sits with Gae and me for the second part. Miracle. Absolute miracle.

ONE OF YOU HAS A FRIEND

At one point in *Luke 11*, Jesus says to his disciples, "Suppose one of you has a friend, and he goes to him at midnight and he says, 'Friend, lend me three loaves of bread because a friend of mine on a journey has come to me, and I have nothing to set before him.'

"Then the one inside answers, 'Don't bother me, the door is already locked and my children are in bed with me. I can't get up and give you anything.' I tell you, though he will not get up and give him the bread because he is his friend, yet because of the man's persistence (or "boldness" in other translations) he will get up and give him as much as he needs" (*v. 5-8*).

I think of how many of my prayers go unanswered because I simply give up. I knock once or twice and then I figure, "He must be asleep." And I go home. Prayers about really important things in my life: prayers about my kids, prayers for my wife and our marriage, prayers for friends or other family members, prayers for things in our ministry—staff people, places, resources, kids, camp, leaders, issues we are dealing with—pretty important stuff.

ASK

"So I say to you: Ask and it will be given to you; seek and you will find; knock and the door will be opened to you. For everyone who asks, receives; he who seeks finds; and to him who knocks, the door will be opened" (*v. 9-10*).

He loves us so deeply and so wants to give us all that we hope for and desire. Richard Rohr says, "So make sure you desire, desire deeply, desire yourself, desire God, desire everything good, true, and beautiful," because God wants to give you those things. "God, like nature," Rohr says, "abhors all vacuums and rushes to fill them" (*Falling Upward, p. 160*). And he fills them with his goodness.

I am not sure why Jesus set it up this way, but he wants us to ask, and he wants us to persist in asking. He wants us to persevere, not only in life but also in our wanting, our desiring, our hoping, and our desperate trusting that he will come through.

He says, "Which of you fathers, if your son asks for a fish will give him a snake instead? Or if he asks for an egg, will give him a scorpion? If you then, who are evil, know how to give good gifts to your children, how much more will your Father in heaven give the Holy Spirit to those who ask him?"

God is good. He is good. And he is good in a much bigger way than we are good. As a dad, I love my kids. If they ask me for something, and it makes sense, I want to give it to them. Even sometimes when it doesn't make sense, I will give it to them. How much more, how much more, does our Father in heaven want to give us good gifts?

NOT EASY

Unfortunately, perseverance is not always easy to come by. It usually is produced through some sort of suffering, and suffering can be hard. Paul says in Romans: "Not only so, but we also rejoice in our sufferings, because we know that suffering produces perseverance; perseverance, character; and character, hope" (*Romans 5:3-4*). Paul knew that in order to have the strength to endure and persevere we must exercise some of those muscles through suffering.

The good side is that perseverance then produces character

and character produces hope. And hope is what allows us to keep going when things seem dark and hopeless.

WORTH IT?

In Hebrews it says that we should "run with perseverance the race marked out for us" (*Hebrews 12:1*). Which implies this race won't be easy. There will be obstacles. There will be difficulties.

Your child will sit on the sidewalk and refuse to get up. You will get frustrated. You will want to quit. You will wonder, and maybe wonder often, "Is this really worth it?"

And then, if you are like us, you will look back years later, like in the case of our church, and think, *Thank goodness we didn't give up. Thank goodness we hung in there. Thank goodness God didn't let us leave.* They have been so good to us, literally "springs of living water," through gut-splitting adjustments for us and our kids, through our desperate attempts to find community and rhythm in this frantic city, through trying to navigate our new surroundings and new job. And then, as we were finally about to gain our footing—Gae begins an almost year-long battle with cancer. We would not have made it without them, plain and simple. We would have left. We would have quit. We would have gone home. And God knew that.

So when you are sitting out on the sidewalk and it is entering the eighth month and you are freezing your bottom off and not much has changed and your son won't move and you are beginning to wonder, "What are we doing here? Is this worth it? Does God see us? Does anyone see us?" And you are knocking on the door and you feel like no one hears you, and the voice inside is saying, "Don't bother me, the door is already locked, and my children are in bed with me. I can't get up and give you anything," then remember, simply remember, Jesus says, "Keep knocking. Keep knocking. Please, keep knocking." And eventually "he will get up and give you as much as you need."

"Consider it pure joy, my brothers and sisters, when you face trials of many kinds, because you know the testing of your faith develops perseverance. Perseverance must finish its work so that you may be mature and complete, not lacking anything" (*James 1:2-4*).

And finish the work.

JOURNAL

Where has life been hard for you recently? Where do you feel you are being tested? Where would you honestly just want to give up?

_____

_____

_____

_____

_____

How does Jesus challenge his disciples to persist in asking? What does he say will happen when we ask? Is he good? Does he desire, more than we do, good things for his children?

_____

_____

_____

_____

_____

Where do you now need to persevere? What do you need to continue to ask him about? How do feel your perseverance is producing character and hope?

_____

_____

_____

_____

_____

PRAY

Dear Jesus, thank you that as a man you knew suffering and you knew perseverance. Thank you that you never give up. Thank you, Jesus, that you are good, that you hear us, and that you want us to come to you and ask and ask boldly. Give us hope. Give us courage. Give us "a sign today of your goodness."

25

Swings

"Remain in me, and I will remain in you" (John 15:4).

READ

Psalm 118
John 15:1-17

SILENCE.

When David was very little, itty-bitty, even before he could walk, he loved to swing. He could swing for hours, as long as you could push him and then some. He loved the motion. His face would just light up when he got in a swing. He loved it even more if you made faces or "peek-a-booed" him or walked in front and then dodged out of the way at the last minute.

David is now seventeen. He still loves swings. Loves them. We were in the park yesterday and went to our favorite playground at the bottom of the park where they have the big swings and the big tire swings. Oh my goodness, David loves the tire swing.

We have a whole routine at this playground that takes over an hour before we actually get to the swings. We start in the little kid area that has a couple of small sliding boards, a huge sand box, some smaller swings, and a little water feature. David gets bored here fairly quickly.

BIG BOY

Then it is off to the big boy part where they have giant sprinklers and water sprayers, tunnels, a huge crater of a rock to climb on, a huge long slide, and then finally, the swings. It takes us anywhere from a half an hour to forty-five minutes to get through this part.

David loves climbing the rock and finds a different path and a heightened degree of difficulty each time we do it. Generally it goes something like this. We walk to what to mc looks like a cliff, and he says, "This way."

I say, "No, if you try to climb up that way you are going to fall and hurt yourself."

To which he replies without fail, "Daddy, do it."

SWINGS

Once we get to the swings, he is raring to go. He runs to an empty swing and then starts jumping or attempting to jump up into it (he hasn't quite gotten down the coordination of jumping up and slightly back at the same time so as to end up on the swing, so I often help).

Then comes the routine. I act like I am Peyton Manning, barking out signals as David sits on the swing in front of me, grinning from ear to ear, anticipating what is coming. "Blue! 92! Blue! 92! Set! Hut one, hut two," I say as I take off running at David, hitting him squarely in the mid section with my shoulder driving him backwards and upwards at the same time and running all the way "through the tackle." He comes flying down, letting out a big scream, and we are off, swinging in pure delight.

He will swing until I stop pushing. We could be there all day if we wanted to (or let's say I wanted to). Once we finish at the big swings it's over to the tire swing. Because there are only two of them, the tire swings tend to have a line, so we can't swing there as long. But David amazes kids and adults. I can almost swing him horizontally on the tire swing, whipping around and around, and he just laughs and holds on, never seems to get dizzy or motion sick or wobbly—just grinning, laughing, making silly noises, laughing at me, laughing at the other kids, and having a blast.

RHYTHM

There is a certain rhythm to the swing that brings it power. I think David feels that rhythm and balance. So much of life and of nature is built around a similar rhythm. I think of the rhythm of our heart or our breath, the rhythm of the waves at the beach, or the tides in the ocean. There is a rhythm to the seasons, winter and summer, the day and the night, the sun and moon, resting and waking, working and sleeping, going out and coming in, gathering and releasing. Life is lived in rhythm.

I am currently sitting at my desk in my room at the Holy Cross Monastery along the Hudson in West Park, NY. As I spoke with one of the brothers yesterday he said, "The rhythm of the monastic life frees me to be with Jesus at deeper and deeper levels."

Prayers mark each day at 7 a.m., 9 a.m., 12 p.m., 5 p.m., and 8 p.m. It is simple and strong, deep and powerful. As you enter in, you feel your body at rest, your mind and heart beginning to focus, the worries and cares of the world beginning to drift apart, your anxious thoughts starting to melt, and the opportunity is there for your soul to drink from deep, powerful, fresh, restoring waters.

RUN

I like to run. I have run maybe four to five times a week now for close to forty years. There is a rhythm to running that puts my mind to rest. I pray best when I run. I think best. The constant motion, the back and forth, the repetitive, physical nature—I tell people often, "Running for me is as much exercise for the mind as it is for the heart."

Ruth Haley Barton in her book, *Strengthening the Soul of your Leadership*, says: "There is nothing (nothing), more crucial to the staying power of the leader than establishing rhythms that keep us replenished—body, mind, and soul. There is nothing more crucial than rhythms that help us make ourselves available to God for the work that only he can do in us—day in and day out. Week in and week out. Year in and year out. All organisms follow life-sustaining rhythms. If we believe that we are somehow above or beyond or immune to our need for such rhythms, we will find ourselves in danger."

JESUS

The life of Jesus was marked by rhythm, by in and out, ebb and flow. Maybe my favorite image is found in *John 15* where he starts by saying, "I am the true vine, and my Father is the gardener" (*v. 1*). He continues, "Abide in me"—"remain in me" as the NIV puts it—and I will abide in you" (*v. 4*). He then goes on to say, "As the Father has loved me, so have I loved you. Now remain, abide, in my love" (*v. 9*).

One way we "remain" in him is by keeping a healthy rhythm to our lives. We have daily rhythms of work and rest, weekly rhythms, yearly, and maybe even for some of us, a seven-year rhythm.

SABBATH

One of the disciplines that I have fought for most recently is that of keeping a weekly Sabbath. With the onslaught of 11 a.m. Sunday soccer games, play practice, baseball games, ministry obligations, meetings, chores to do, people to see, the constant barrage of e-mails and texts, and just plain "not enough time in the day," the idea of a weekly rest or Sabbath for most of us feels darn near impossible.

Peter Scazzero in his book *Emotionally Healthy Spirituality* says, "Sabbath, when lived, is our means as the people of God to bear witness to the way we understand life, its rhythms, its gifts, its meaning, and its ultimate purpose in God. Observing the Sabbath, we affirm: 'God is the center and source of our lives. He is the beginning and the middle and the end of our existence'" (*p. 165*). By keeping the Sabbath and keeping it holy we are saying: "We are not in control. We trust God to provide and care for us. It doesn't all depend on me."

We work six days and we rest for one. It is how God formed the earth. It is how he formed us. To do so is to enter into ancient rhythms of power and grace. It is to abide. It is to trust. And it is to remain. It is to laugh, to rest . . . to swing.

JOURNAL

Where in your life have you felt a sense of powerful rhythm—
at the beach, at the park, when you work, when you run?

_____

_____

_____

_____

_____

How did Jesus keep these rhythms sacred? How did he work
and rest? How did he balance times with the crowd and times of
solitude and silence?

_____

_____

_____

_____

What comes to mind when you think of this idea of "abiding
in Jesus"? How does the Sabbath play a part in that abiding?
What gets in the way of you resting each week?

_____

_____

_____

_____

_____

PRAY

_Jesus, thank you for the rhythms of life—sun, moon, light,
darkness, morning, evening. Thank you for how you both
worked and rested. I trust you with each day and each week,
the chance to work and the chance to rest. You are in control.
You can do this without me. Give me strength and courage to
establish rhythms that keep me replenished—body, mind, and
soul._

26

Unpredictable

*"The wind blows wherever it pleases. You hear its sound,
but you cannot tell where it comes from or where it is going.
So it is with everyone born of the Spirit" (John 3:8).*

READ

Psalm 104
Matt 14:13-21

SILENCE.

When I think of David, often the word *unpredictable* comes to mind. In almost every situation you have to think, *Not sure how this is going to work, but here we go.* Living life with David is living every day as an adventure; you just are never sure what will happen next.

The subways in New York can also be an adventure. When we first moved here it maybe took us three or four months before we considered a subway ride with David. There are just too many variables—tracks, electric current, voltage, fast-moving trains, loud noises, people having really bad days, crowds, crowded cars, turnstiles, stairs, trains that go in the wrong direction, local, express, multiple tracks, letters, numbers, colors—you name it.

So we waited. And we got comfortable with it. And then one day we thought, "Okay, I think we're ready. We can do this."

Typically the routine would be that Gae or I would swipe in, go through the turnstile, and wait, eyes peeled on David, hands outstretched. The other person would then swipe David in, be sure he was safely in the hands of the first person, and then quickly swipe in and come through, all the while never fully losing contact with David. We would find a seat and wait for a train. Perfect. No worries.

Our greatest fear is that David would either get on a train without us or we would get on a train and leave him standing there on the platform. Both of those scenarios made us nauseous.

So this one day, not too very long ago, David and I were out, just the two of us. And I thought, *I can handle this. I just need to be careful.* So David and I headed for the subway.

1 TRAIN

It was the 1 Train headed downtown, which, coming from the Upper West Side, can be crowded even on a weekend. I had my metro card and I was prepared. We get downstairs; I have David with me, so far so good. I swipe him in, he goes through the turnstile, and I say, "Wait right there!" As soon as I say that a train pulls up, and David gets this little twinkle in his eye. Gae's not there, the doors on the train open, and I say, "Wait!"

He runs onto the train, and at that point I begin to panic. I am fumbling with my metro card, trying to get through the turnstile, people on the train are looking at me and then looking at David, then looking at me, and he has this really silly grin on his face, knowing he was doing something naughty but thinking, "This is the most fun I have ever had."

All I can think is, *Gae is going to kill me.*

So I hurdle the turnstile. Hurdle it. Try to think Edwin Moses, '84 Olympics in Los Angeles. Have that picture in your mind. I clear the turnstile by maybe eight inches, I sprint the last twenty or twenty-five feet as the little bell dings and the subway doors begin to close, and I literally do a "superman" into the subway car, headfirst, arms extended, full-length dive, and land right at David's feet. He is in hysterics. He can't laugh any harder. He's about to wet his pants. He thinks this is hilarious.

People are looking at him, looking at me, looking at him. "Wow, that was incredible." And I think, *I am way too old for this.*

SOLITARY PLACE

Living life with Jesus is nothing if it isn't unpredictable. In *Matthew 14*, Jesus hears that John the Baptist had been beheaded, and it says, "He withdrew by boat privately to a solitary place." Now if I had done that, I would be there pretty much by myself in a solitary place. Not so with Jesus.

Jesus goes to a solitary place and five thousand people show up.

And as they arrive it says Jesus sees the crowd and "has compassion on them." He gets out of the boat and starts healing their sick and teaching them (*Mark 6:34*). Are you serious? If there was one day you thought he might say, "You know guys, not today. I am really tired. Can we dismiss the crowd? I need a little break here." But he doesn't.

FIVE BARLEY LOAVES AND TWO FISH

As evening approached, the disciples came and said, "This is a remote place, and it's getting late, send them away so they can get something to eat." And this is where it gets crazy.

"They do not need to go away," Jesus replied. "You give them something to eat."

Really? Philip looks over this crowd and says, "Eight months wages would not buy enough bread for each person to have a bite" (*John 6:7*). He's not wrong, but he's just not thinking of Jesus.

Andrew, Peter's brother, says, "Here's a boy with five small barley loaves and two small fish." Which is a nice thing to say, but have you checked out the crowd lately? Five loaves and two fish?

Jesus says, "Bring them here to me." Okay, and then what? And he tells everyone to sit down, and he gives thanks, breaks the loaves, and gives them to the disciples to give to the people.

I love the fact that the disciples participate, that Jesus wants them to be a part of this miracle. They are in on this, and it is their hands and feet that pass out the fish and the bread. They aren't confused on who is performing this miracle or where all this bread is coming from, and they certainly can't take credit for it. But they get to play a part.

I'm also not sure anyone in the crowd knew where all the bread and fish came from. I'm not sure it mattered. But the disciples knew.

SATISFIED

"They all ate until they were satisfied" (*Matthew 14:20*). That is so great. *Psalm 104* says that every living thing "looks to you to give them their food at the proper time." Can you imagine being God and every day waking up thinking, "There are a lot of things out there that need to eat today."

Then it says, "You open your hand and they are satisfied with good things" (*Ps 104:27-28*). You open your hand?! That's all it takes? Yep. God opens his hand and we are satisfied . . . with *good* things.

And the disciples picked up twelve baskets of broken pieces that were left over, twelve! That is amazing. "The number of those who ate was about five thousand men, besides women and children." He fed an army.

ALL IN

I am not sure we like *unpredictable* in our culture. Unpredictable is uncomfortable. Unpredictable is messy. Unpredictable feels out of control. If you aren't careful, unpredictable can get you killed. It's like spending the day in the city with David. You have to be watching at all times. You can't relax even for a second. And even with that, you may still have to hurdle the turnstile and do a superman at a moments notice.

The disciples spent every day like that, having no idea what was next—when they might get a chance to sit down and rest, when they would be out in a boat, when they would be walking along the road, when Jesus would stop and heal a blind man, raise a dead man, or sit next to a women at the well. Or when they would go to a solitary place and five thousand people might just show up. Everyday was a crazy adventure. They had no clue. They could only trust. They were all in, no way of going back, burned the boats, lost it all, left everything, fully in, and completely sold out. Bonhoffer says it like this:

They have no security, no possessions to call their own, not even a foot of earth to call their home, no earthly society to claim their absolute allegiance. Nay more, they have no spiritual power, experience or knowledge to afford them consolation or security. For his sake they have lost all. In following him, they lost even their own selves, and everything that could make them rich. Now they are poor—so inexperienced, so stupid, that they have no other hope but him who called them. (*Cost of Discipleship*)

What a scary place to be. What a great place to be.

JOURNAL

Think of a time in your life where something happened you didn't expect; something you felt was completely unpredictable? How did you feel? What was happening around you? What were others saying?

_____

_____

_____

_____

_____

On that day in *Matthew 14*, who thought that huge crowd would show up? How does Jesus react? What do the disciples think should happen? How are they stunned by what Jesus does?

_____

_____

_____

_____

_____

What in your life right now feels unpredictable or out of your control? Where is God asking you to trust fully, completely, all in trust him for what happens next? How does it feel to do that?

_____

_____

_____

_____

_____

PRAY

Jesus, I fully and completely trust you. Life can be crazy, out of control, unpredictable. You are good. You want the best for me. The only solid ground available is in you and with you. All else is shifting sand. I land both of my feet in with you. Direct my steps. I will follow. I am yours—heart, mind, body, and soul.

27

Plop

*"Since they could not get him to Jesus because
of the crowd . . . " (Mark 2:4).*

READ

Psalm 34
Mark 2:1-12

SILENCE.

When David doesn't like something, or is simply registering his displeasure, he sits down wherever he is, could be on the floor or the sidewalk, in a crowded room or, on occasion, in the middle of the street.

As I talked about in "Being His Advocate," our first attempt at finding David a school in New York was a modest disaster. It really just never worked. So, by the end of October, we were back to the drawing board.

And for over a month we waited, thinking we might hear something from the Department of Education. We applied to various private schools with little or no luck. We even went back to the first school that had initially rejected us. In every case, it either wasn't a good fit or they were full.

Gae tried home schooling. Oh man. Even David knew that was a bad idea.

As the frustration grew, seeds of doubt began to mushroom into full-blown jungles. In our own way, without ever really saying it, I think we both began to wonder if we had missed it and this whole move to New York was one whopping big mistake.

REBECCA

And then we found the Rebecca School. What a God send. A small private school whose mission is kids like David, who has as their school motto: "Learning through Relationships." Wow. We signed him up. And his first day would be the day after Thanksgiving break.

He had been out of school for over a month and grown accustomed to waking up and coming out and just sitting on the couch. Sounds familiar. So for the next week, Gae and I plotted on what that first day would look like, how we would prep him, lay out his clothes, get started early, pack his lunch, take him to the train, and talk about "going on an adventure."

FIND MOMMY

We decided that Gae would leave first, and the game would be "let's go find Mommy." And Mommy would just happen to be sitting right in front of David's new school. So, around 7:30 a.m. that first morning, Gae left. She headed for the train while I waited with David.

At around 7:45 I said, "Let's go find Mommy." He refused. This wasn't in the plan. We didn't think our first hurdle would be getting him out of the house. For twenty minutes I tried everything. "I'll buy you a milkshake." "When we get home, I'll take you to a movie." "Mommy is lonely." "Mommy is lost." He was having none of it. So, finally, I called Gae and said, "Forget it, come on home. He isn't budging."

Two seconds later, he jumps up and says, "I'm ready." I'm stunned. So we put on his backpack and head out the door. In my excitement I forgot to call Gae back.

We are getting on the train and all of the sudden I think, *Oh crap, we are going to find Mommy, but Mommy isn't there anymore.* So as soon as I get off the train I call Gae and say, "Turn around, we are heading for the school."

ON A MISSION

For some reason, at this point, David is on a mission. He starts walking like he lost his dog. We are less than a block from the school when I text Gae and say, "Where are you?"

"I just got off the train."

"Run!" I say.

Just as I put down the phone, David plops down on the sidewalk and says, "All done."

"All done?" We still have a block to go.

Nope. He's sitting down. Not to mention he is sitting in the middle of the sidewalk at the corner of 30th and Madison, one of the busiest corners in Manhattan at 8:20 a.m. on a Monday morning. There are literally hundreds of people stepping over him, trying to walk around him, looking at me like, "What are you doing with this child?"

At one point a cab stops and the cabbie rolls down his window and says, "Can I help you?"

And I say, "I am trying to get him to school."

He says, "I can get him to school."

I believed him. I just didn't have the guts to get in the back of the cab and say, "Yeah, just about one hundred fifty yards or so down the street, please."

Finally, out of the corner of my eye, I see Gae sprinting down the sidewalk on the other side of the street. Now that's funny. Weaving her way in and out of people. Trying to get there ahead of us. I say, "Slow it down. He's not moving." Gae, completely out of breath, comes back and joins us on the corner. After twenty minutes coercing, prodding, and just plain sitting in traffic, she decides to go get one of the teachers from the school and see if they can help us.

READY AND EAGER

Out springs a young, vivacious, ready-for-battle, eager, twenty-something-year-old female teacher who brings out one of their rolling office chairs. She looks at David and says, "Would you like to push me?"

He thinks, "Wow, what kind of game is this?" She jumps in the chair and off they go down the sidewalk.

After fifteen or twenty feet she jumps up and says, "Can I push you?"

"Sure!" David jumps in the chair, she wraps her arms around him, and all three of us start running with him to the school— straight down the sidewalk. People are going airborne to get out of the way. Briefcases and lunchboxes flying up in the air, office workers diving against car doors, cheering us on, David laughing, and we're all screaming.

We get to the school and the staff waiting for us opens the doors just as we get there, and we roll him right into the lobby. We are laughing, crying, hugging, and completely out of breath. Finally, Gae and I look at each other, look at the teacher, slap her high five, give her the thumbs up, and say, "Good luck. Call us." And we head for breakfast. God is good.

A GUY WITH A VISION

As I think of this story of David, I can only think of the story of the paralytic in *Mark 2*. Here on what could have been a fairly warm and dusty afternoon, a guy has a vision. "If we get "Jimmy" to the feet of Jesus, I believe he can heal him, forever. I believe it." So this guy goes and gets three of his friends. "Hey, come help me carry Jimmy to the feet of Jesus."

"Wow, what a great idea," they think, and off they go.

As they get to the house, they realize how crowded it is. People are standing in the doorway, hanging out the windows, jammed in the living room. And it dawns on them. "We may not be able to get Jimmy in the door."

UP ON THE ROOF

This is probably my favorite part of the story. One of the guys, as they are standing there outside of the house still out of breathe, wondering what to do next, has to look up and say, "Why don't we take him up on the roof?"

"What?"

"Why don't we take him up on the roof?"

"Oh, that's a good idea. Then what?"

"We'll tear a hole in it."

"What?"

"We'll tear a hole in it."

"Are you nuts?"

All the while Jimmy is lying there thinking, "If you drop me, man, I am going to kill you, man."

What I like so much about this part of the story is that these guys could have just packed it in at that point. It would have been easy to think, "We should have come earlier," or, "Maybe Jesus will be back tomorrow," or, "Why don't we just write him a note and ask him to stop by on his way home?"

But they didn't. They weren't willing to take no for an answer. They believed, with all their hearts, that if they could just get Jimmy to Jesus, Jesus could heal him. It would be a miracle. But they believed it. And they weren't about to let a crowd of people or a roof or the fact that they needed now to go find some rope stop them.

START DIGGING

So they head for the roof. And they start digging, and not a little hole I might add, a six-foot by four-foot hole, and they begin to lower Jimmy down. Jesus looks up, and the scripture says, "Seeing their faith." Jesus knew what a risk this was. He knew these guys could have left and gone home or simply waited for Jesus to be done. He knew what other people sitting there might be thinking. None of that stopped these guys, and Jesus knew it.

And Jesus looks at Jimmy and says, "My son (I love that), your sins are forgiven." Jesus knows that the first thing that needs to be healed is this boy's heart—he needs to be forgiven, to be whole, to wipe away any shame or guilt. Even more than his legs, it's his heart.

And then Jesus says, "Just so you know the Son of Man has authority on earth to forgive sins, take up your pallet and walk." And so, Jimmy did.

Can you begin to imagine what it would have been like to be there that day and to witness all this? The guys coming to the door not being able to get in, hearing the footsteps up on the roof, beginning to see dirt and straw and bits of tile falling down on Jesus as he spoke, and then this paralytic being lowered from the ceiling? Are you kidding?

FOUR GUYS

But then think of the four guys who brought him. Now that was outrageous. They didn't walk out, as the teacher at David's school could have, and say, "Well if you can't get him to come in, I guess he can't go to school here." No, they brought a chair with them and started wheeling him down the sidewalk. They got crazy and creative. They took a massive risk and actually dug up someone's roof. They did property damage just to get this kid to the feet of Jesus.

And then they walked home with their arms around Jimmy, carrying his pallet, smacking high fives, thinking, "That was awesome. That was really awesome."

JOURNAL

Can you think of a time when you were stuck, weren't really sure what to do, needed to get creative, take a risk, or do something out of the ordinary?

_____

_____

_____

_____

_____

Why do you think these guys refused to take no for an answer? What did Jesus notice about them? Who benefited from the fact that they didn't give up?

_____

_____

_____

_____

_____

What might God be calling you to now that seems difficult? At what point would you turn back or give up? How is he calling you to be creative and take a risk?

_____

_____

_____

_____

_____

PRAY

Jesus, life is hard and ministry is hard. It is easy to want to give up sometimes. Give me courage. Help me to be creative. Give me a partner or two who will go with me, who will not only encourage me, but will get up on the roof with me. Allow me, in the face of all odds, to be fearless, to trust you and trust you fully and to not give up or go home until our friend gets to "the feet of Jesus."

28

Holy Ambition

*"Peter asked, 'Lord, why can't I follow you now?
I will lay down my life for you'" (John 13:37).*

READ

Psalm 127
John 13:31-38

SILENCE.

David reached a milestone the other day. He dressed himself for the first time. His mom and I were ecstatic. He was sixteen.

As a dad, especially as a driven dad who easily measures everything by performance, you have certain expectations for your kids—do well in school, perform well in sports, thrive in extracurricular activities, make good friends, get into a good college, get a good job, love your mom and dad, provide for us in old age.

As much as we hate to admit it, our children are a reflection of us as parents. And so when our kids do well, we do well. We easily find ourselves living our lives through theirs.

DRIVEN

From the day I was born, I wanted to be president of the United States of America. When we picked teams in the backyard in elementary school, I always chose first. I appointed myself quarterback. If it was baseball, I was the pitcher or the shortstop. I never played right field.

The first chance I had to run for president, I did. I was a junior in high school. I ran again my senior year. I was class president for the second year in a row. I was captain of the football team and the baseball team, and not because I was good but because I wanted it. I worked hard and I hustled.

I got to college and I had become a Christian, so I became a small-group leader, then the large-group leader, then part of the executive team. Every group, gathering, club, or sport I was a part of, I led. To God be the glory.

When I graduated from college, I joined the Young Life staff and became a club leader, then an area director, then a regional director, and now a senior vice president. God is proud of me. So am I.

PETER

I love Peter. I guess if I could be anybody in the Bible, I'd be Peter. I would ask Jesus to call me out on the water. I would want to build tabernacles for Jesus, Moses, and Elijah. I would speak before I knew what I was saying. I would throw on my clothes and jump over the side of the boat. I would ask Jesus to wash not just my feet but also my whole body. I would kneel in a boatload of fish, and I would cut off the ear of one of the temple guards if they tried to arrest Jesus. I would do all of that.

I would also say this, "Lord, why can't I follow you now? I will lay down my life for you."

And I think I might also hear Jesus say, "Will you really lay down your life for me? I tell you the truth, before the rooster crows, you will disown me three times" (*John 13:37-38*).

That had to hurt. Peter so desperately wanted to please. He wanted Jesus to love him. He wanted to be first, he wanted to step out, he wanted to take the lead, and he wanted Jesus and the rest to know he was "all in."

But it was all wrong.

Motivation is so important, the *why* about what we are doing, not just the *what*. With this move to New York, I have over and over again needed to ask myself, "Who is this about, really? Why do I want to do this? Why so desperately do I want this to work? Who ultimately gets the glory here? It's a great story, but who is the story about, really?"

Jesus is saying to Peter, "I love you. I really do. But this isn't going to be about you now. This is going to be about me. This is going to be about my glory and my father's glory. Not yours."

HOLY AMBITION

I do think there is such a thing as holy ambition. I think God often puts things in our hearts to do, big things, things he is not asking anyone else to do, important things. But it needs to be at the right time and for the right reasons.

Paul, in one of my favorite verses of all time, says to the Thessalonians, "We loved you so much that we were delighted to share with you not only the gospel of God but our lives as well because you had become so dear to us." He says it is hard work. "You remember our toil and hardship; we worked night and day in order to not be a burden to anyone while we preached the gospel of God to you" (*I Thess. 2:8-9*).

I am sure he wanted the Thessalonians to come to Jesus, lots of them. He wanted big clubs with tons of kids and large camp trips. He wanted to establish a church there, and he wanted it to thrive—just like he did in Ephesus and Philippi and Corinth and Colossae. He worked night and day for crying out loud.

But for who's glory, for who's credit, for what or who's recognition? Was it so that people might think he's a great speaker or small-group leader or writer or the kind of guy who gets it done?

He says, "We are not trying to please men but God, who tests our hearts. We were not looking for praise from men, not from you or anyone else" (*v. 4,6*). Was it hard at times? I am sure it was. Did he have bad days? I'm sure he did. Did he wonder even if he had made a mistake? Probably. But at the core there was freedom. He knew this wasn't about him. Or them.

THE END OF OURSELVES

Just because we are so deceitful, so easily self-focused without even knowing it, we can want to do the right thing for all the wrong reasons. And because that is true, God has a way of letting us get to the end of ourselves—to that point of utter surrender where all that we have done up to that point to keep ourselves replenished and grounded no longer works, where a longer *quiet time* or another walk in the park or getting up thirty minutes earlier or going on one more long run is just not enough, where we are completely out of gas—done. And we simply throw ourselves into the arms of the loving God and say, "Help me. Help me, Daddy."

Moses, I believe, had a God-given desire to rescue the Israelites from the hands of the Egyptians. From the time he was a baby, he thought about it and wanted to do it. But the day he killed an Egyptian for beating one of his fellow Hebrews, God sent him into the wilderness for forty years to tend sheep. David had to be confronted by Nathan, Paul was knocked from his horse, Peter denied Jesus three times and wept bitterly, and Nehemiah experienced the exile of his people and the destruction of Jerusalem.

There is always a certain amount of brokenness, of undoing, of unlearning and relearning that allows us to get to a place where God can actually use us.

Richard Rohr says, "Until you bottom out and come to the limits of your own fuel supply, there is no reason for you to switch to a higher octane of fuel. In fact, you will not even know there is a Larger Source until your own sources and resources fail you" (*Breathing Underwater, p. 3*).

That is a scary and a hard place, but a necessary place—and God often allows us to get there.

KEEPING ME HONEST

David keeps me honest. He helps me to think right. Instead of tweaking my idea of *success*, I've had to throw out the whole book and start over.

Life is simpler: good bowl of chips and hummus, a big plate of spaghetti, a ride on the tandem, a trip to the playground, an afternoon with his mom and dad. It's almost like he's saying, "You know, Dad, all that stuff you think about and worry about, it's okay. God's got that. And he gave you me to prove it."

JOURNAL

Think of a time when you did something or accomplished something that you were proud of. How did you feel? What made you feel that way?

_____

_____

_____

_____

_____

In what ways do you see Peter as ambitious? How does Jesus let him get to the end of himself? How does that help him in the long run?

_____

_____

_____

_____

_____

What do you hear God calling you to do? How do you struggle between doing it for God's glory and doing it for your own recognition? What would it take for you to switch to a "higher octane of fuel?"

_____

_____

_____

_____

_____

PRAY

Thank you, Jesus, that you are a God of big dreams and big resources. Thank you that throughout history you have called men and women to really big things. Help us, Jesus. Help this to not be about us—our glory, our recognition, our need for praise, our desire to please, our fear of failure. Let it be your power, your resources, your strength, your desire, your heart, and your Spirit, that in the end the glory and the praise would be all yours, dear Jesus.

29

Slow it Down

"But only one thing is needed. Mary has chosen what is better"
(Luke 10:42).

READ

Psalm 27
Luke 10:38-42

SILENCE.

Our culture worships speed. Faster is simply better. Fast cars, fast planes, fast internet, fast food, fast readers, fast thinkers, fast walkers, and fast talkers. More projects getting done quicker and faster. Lightening speed apps get us more information faster. Weather, sports, Google, Facebook, news, stock market, pictures, maps, directions, games—with a touch of a button we can update ourselves on everything and anything imaginable. We simply don't have time to wait.

PACE

Life with David moves at a different pace. When we walk somewhere, even just around the block, it may take us twice as long as it would if I were going alone. David often stops to say hello to strangers. He looks in shops and at the people in the restaurants. Squirrels, trees, birds, and the wind distract him. He even stops sometimes and just sits down.

If I were to define my life apart from David, one word that might come to mind would be: *hurry*. I hurry to the grocery store. I hurry to work. I hurry to get home. I hurry to church. I hurry to get around people who walk too slowly on the sidewalk or who are moving slowly down the steps into the subway. I always look for the shortest checkout line or the fastest lane on the highway because I am in a hurry. I text while I'm walking.

It saves me time. I return messages while I'm checking email. I take a 24-hour day and pack fifty-two hours worth of stuff into it. It makes me feel better.

I wonder if Jesus was ever in a hurry? I think about the encounters he had with Bartimaeus or the woman at the well or the woman caught in adultery or the woman with the issue of blood or the centurion or the leper or the rich young ruler. Would any of those people say, "I just felt like he was in a hurry. He kind of just rushed past me. He seemed distracted." How much would he have missed, or more importantly, would we have missed, if he ran through life like I do?

MARY AND MARTHA

Today we see Jesus on the road with his disciples. He is invited to stop at the home of Mary and Martha for lunch. As we read the account of Lazarus in *John 11* we see that Jesus was a very close friend of this family. My guess is this was a regular stop for him.

But this time Martha seems to be doing all the work: running here and there, getting the dishes out, setting the table, fixing the salad, heating up the green beans and the fried chicken, making sure everyone has plenty to drink. Meanwhile, her sister Mary is simply sitting there enjoying listening to Jesus.

Finally Martha has had enough. She pops. She comes to Jesus and simply blurts out, "Lord, don't you care that my sister has left me to do the work by myself? Tell her to help me!"

Wow. Do I feel like that sometimes? Why am I doing all the work? Is anyone else in on this? Doesn't it feel like I am doing more than my share? Does anyone care as much as I do? If it's going to get done, am I always the one who has to do it? Does it always depend on me?! Can I get a little more help over here?!

Jesus replied, "Martha, Martha, you are worried and upset about many things. But only one thing is needed. Mary has chosen what is better, and it won't be taken away from her."

DISTRACTION

I live a life of distraction. There is always so much to do, so much to get done. If Martha isn't there that day, they don't eat. Somebody has to get the plates on the table, warm up the bread, cook the beans, and pour the tea. So people like Martha and me, we get it done.

Which on the one hand is a good thing. I get a lot done. I am a doer. I like feeling like I've accomplished something. People give me a lot because they know I'll get it done. I like a lot of checks on my checklist. I often get noticed, even praised, for what I can accomplish.

On the other hand, I never slow down. I don't know what it's like to take a breath. I don't have a resting heart beat. I don't know "what is better" because I don't slow down long enough to figure it out.

I start every day with a blank slate, even Saturday and vacation days. I am literally running from one thing to the next. Achievement is an idol. Performance is my god.

Which often leads to what is commonly called *burnout*.

Here's how my friend Fil Anderson describes it:

I was more than busy; I was exhausted. At night I was restless— too many of the day's activities would loop through my brain. And the following morning it was all I could do to drag myself out of bed to face the day. I was running on grit and adrenaline. For quite some time I had loved having every moment crammed with activity. More specifically, it was the fuel on which I ran. I loved being in demand. But now I was running on empty. (*Running on Empty, p. 4*)

RUN HARDER

A good friend of mine, Jerry Leachman, has said more than once, "Only a third, a third, of all Christian leaders finish well." A third! That is mind blowing to me. My guess is that many of us get to where Fil was and we can't get any further. We don't know a way out. Like me, they have believed a few things that simply aren't true. Things like: we are immune; the rules don't apply to us; we are needed; we are way too important. "I need to be there for that." "I'm really the only one who can do that." "This is why I'm here." "God called me."

And so, we run. We run. We are pressed. And we push. And the work is never done. And we can never fully quench our thirst. And people praise us. And they say we are such *hard workers* and *great preachers* and we are *getting it done*, and they are seeing such incredible *growth* and *stuff happening* and that makes us happy, and it feels good, like a drug, like *crack* in our veins. Without ever meaning to, we become addicted to it—and so, not knowing what else to do, we just run harder. Until we can't.

God, forgive us.

Forgive me.

Jesus says, "Are you tired? Worn out? Burned out on religion? Come to me. Get away with me and you'll recover your life. I'll show you how to take a real rest. Walk with me and work with me—watch how I do it. Learn the unforced rhythms of grace. I won't lay anything heavy or ill-fitting on you. Keep company with me and you'll learn to live freely and lightly" (*Matt. 11:28-30, MSG*).

SLOW IT DOWN

David helps me to slow down. He helps me to notice. He helps me to realize how much is missed when I am living life at my pace. He brings me a depth and quality that I wouldn't know otherwise. He literally looks at me from time to time and says, "Slow it down."

I think Mary understood that. It's not that what Martha was doing was unimportant, of course it was. But it was, at the time, much less important.

This summer has been a sabbatical rest for me. What a gift. I am realizing for the first time in a long time what happens when you simply alter your pace—you slow it down. Your food tastes better; you eat better; you notice people; you see things; your heart slows down; you sleep better; you listen better; you focus; you are mindful; you don't forget things; you can concentrate; you aren't easily frustrated; people like you; you have a larger *tank*; you are healthy; you are not annoyed; you are intentional; you are hopeful; you are rested; you bring a sense of peace and calm to those around you.

How much is that worth to you? How important are you really?

"Martha, Martha," the Lord answered, "you are worried and upset about many things, but only one thing is needed. Mary has chosen what is better, and it will not be taken away from her."

JOURNAL

At what speed would you say you live your life? Why? What is it that is driving you? What is the cost to that? Who is in charge of your schedule?

_____

_____

_____

_____

_____

What is Jesus trying to say to Martha? Why is she frustrated? Is what Jesus is saying even realistic? Can we really sit at his feet and listen when so many things need to get done?

_____

_____

_____

_____

_____

How would you recalibrate if you could? What would a more sustainable pace look like for you? What would be the benefits of that? What do you need to change in order to get there?

_____

_____

_____

_____

_____

PRAY

Today, Jesus, I trust you for everything that needs to get done. Everything. "Apart from you, I can do absolutely nothing." I believe every part of that. Help me to walk intentionally through the day. Walk, not run. Give me time for those you put in my path, particularly those most dear to me. Give me free moments where I sit to watch and wonder and simply let you love me. I love you, Jesus.

30

Pure Joy

"So we fix our eyes not on what is seen, but what is unseen.
For what is seen is temporary, but what is unseen is eternal"
(II Cor. 4:18).

READ

Psalm 100
Acts 16:16-40

SILENCE.

Happiness is overrated. Happiness is temporary. Happiness is fleeting. It is contingent. Joy is deep, powerful, liberating, has no real connection to what we consider as our *circumstances*. Joy is a choice, it is an opportunity, and it is a part of faith. Joy comes only because we see something bigger, something that outweighs, outlasts, and out performs, something that is more powerful, weightier, and even more real than what is right in front of us.

LEAKING JOY

I think of David and how his joy seems to simply leak out of him. We could be riding bikes or walking in the park or on our way to church or waiting for the bus for school. It is not something he thinks about or concentrates on or makes any real conscious effort to do or to be. He is simply joyful. David's joy is a gift from God. And it is contagious.

Paul says in *II Corinthians 4* that we "have this treasure in jars of clay to show that this all surpassing power is from God and not from us." I do sometimes think that, in a good way, David's jar is a little less put together than say mine is, a little less firm, a little less hard, maybe with some wider and deeper cracks in it that simply allows the joy and the power and the grace and the truth of who Jesus is shine through a bit brighter and a bit more pure.

POT'S BOAT

One of David's favorite things in the whole world is to ride on the tube behind Pots's boat (Pots is David's grandfather, my dad). When he was really little, he would sit in the hole of the tube and Pots would pull him real slow and we would all cheer. His face would simply light up.

Then he got strong enough to hold on to one of us, and he would ride on our backs and Pots would go *fast*. He and Jessi were a great team. He loved it.

Now he rides solo on his own tube. Pots goes fast and David literally hangs on for dear life. And he absolutely loves it. His face explodes with sheer joy. It is almost like he's been set free— the speed of the boat, the motion of the waves, the excitement, the feeling of flying along the water. His hair is whipping in the breeze, the water splashing up behind him, across the wake and back, and he's waving to Mom-mom on the shore, laughing, doing the "superman" every once in a while, giving Pots the thumbs up. "Go faster, go faster." We all cheer. It's hilarious. Pure joy.

PLACE OF PRAYER

In our passage today, Paul and Silas have made their way to Philippi (*Acts 16*). They would, as was their custom, go to the place beside the river that was considered the place of prayer. I think of how important that must have been to routinely go to this place of prayer, not only for those gathered there, but for Paul and Silas.

One day as Paul and Silas were on their way, they met a slave girl who "had a spirit by which she predicted the future" (*v. 16*). This earned her owners a great deal of money.

However, she began following Paul and Silas through the town shouting, "These men are servants of the Most High God, who are telling you the way to be saved." This went on for days. Finally it says Paul became "so troubled" that he turns and says to the spirit, "In the name of Jesus Christ come out of her." Which it did. Immediately.

PRISON

The owners, having lost their primary source of income, become enraged and drag Paul and Silas into the marketplace.

They brought them before the authorities and accused them of throwing the city into an uproar. So the magistrates have them "stripped, beaten, severely flogged, and thrown into jail."

I have never spent a night in jail. I certainly have never spent a night in a first-century Philippian jail. And I can only imagine what it would feel like to be thrown in jail for healing a little slave girl of a hurtful spirit. But there was Paul and Silas. They were stripped and beaten and severely flogged and in prison. They were taken to the inner cell where they chained them to each other and to the wall.

There they sit in what I imagine was utter darkness: no windows, little air to breath, damp, rats, rodents, really hot or really cold, bruised, beaten, bloody, chained to each other and to the wall. And what do they do? The very next verse says, "About midnight Paul and Silas were praying and singing hymns to God." Are you kidding me? Praying and singing hymns? Joy?

Unfortunately, if this were my story, that would not be the very next verse. No, the very next verse would read something like: "And John was mad as fire. Blazing mad. He looked like he was about to tear someone's head off, thinking about how he would get back at those who had done this to him, how he would flog them, how he would make them pay, how he would call his lawyer who was smart and rich, how his parents would be upset and rip someone a new one, how his friends hated when stuff like this happened. And he was angry, unhappy, and frustrated. And he cursed God."

PHILIPPIANS

Philippians, the letter Paul wrote to these same people when he was in another jail, is often referred to as the "Epistle of Joy." The word *joy* appears over sixteen times in four short chapters.

Paul says, "I always pray with joy because of your partnership in the gospel" (1:4).

"Through my being with you again your joy in Christ will overflow" (1:26).

"Make my joy complete" (2:2).

"My brothers, you whom I love and long for, my joy and crown" (4:1).

"Rejoice in the Lord always. I will say it again: Rejoice!" (*4:4*).

Is he nuts? Where does all this joy and rejoicing come from? He's in jail for crying out loud. These same Philippians had him flogged and thrown into their prison. He should be angry and bitter and frustrated and wanting to rip someone's head off.

THE SECRET

So here it is in my estimation. Here's what makes the difference. Paul says, "I know what it is to be in need, and I know what it is to have plenty. I have learned the secret of being content in any and every situation, whether well fed or hungry, whether living in plenty or in want" (*Phil. 4:12-13*).

The secret? What secret? That it is not about you! Paul can be joyful laying there in prison or laying on the beach or when things are great or when things are really not great because for Paul, none of that really matters! God is in charge! God supplies the joy! There is a bigger story! It is not all about Paul! It is "Christ in you," Christ in me that is "the hope of glory" (*Colossians 1:27*).

Paul is grateful to simply play a part. God is doing something much more grand and glorious. He says he counts everything a loss, as rubbish—as dung he says—compared to the surpassing greatness of knowing Christ (*3:8*). Everything else is a *loss*. He is "Christ's ambassador" (*II Corinthians 5:20*). It doesn't get any better than that. The circumstances are merely that, circumstances: opportunities and ingredients for God to show his glory.

DEEPER REALITY

God knew it would be harder for me to fully get this idea of *pure joy*. I would need for it to be a bit more straightforward, a bit more obvious. So he gave me a son who simply can't contain it, a living picture, and a gift of utter and complete joy. It is a glimpse into a deeper reality that we can't see. So . . .

"We fix our eyes not on what is seen, but what is unseen. For what is seen is temporary, but what is unseen is eternal" (*II Corinthians 4:18*).

JOURNAL

Do you consider yourself to be a joyful person? What do you see as the difference between joy and happiness?

_____

_____

_____

_____

_____

What was the source of joy for Paul? How did he remain joyful despite his circumstances?

_____

_____

_____

_____

_____

How much of joy is a matter of focus? How can you keep your focus on Jesus, on what is eternal, despite what is happening around you?

_____

_____

_____

_____

_____

PRAY

O Holy One, today, keep my eyes, my ears, my head, and my heart fixed solely and completely on you, no matter what the world brings my way. Help me, Lord Jesus, to keep my focus on "things eternal" and to be grateful for all you have given me, no matter how large or small, no matter what swirls around me. "The joy of the Lord is indeed my strength." Thank you, dear Jesus.

Epilogue

READ

Psalm 96
John 21:1-18

SILENCE.

There is no resurrection apart from death. There is no rising apart from falling, no light apart from darkness, no dawn apart from night, no spring apart from winter. It is the cycle of all of creation. However, I am certain if you took Gae and me back 17 years , to the weeks and months before David was born, we would not have chosen to have a son born with Down syndrome. We would not have. I am sure of that.

"Death," if you will, is never a choice. The only choice is whether or not you will embrace it and trust it, deny it or dive into it. As Rohr says, "pain is part of the deal." It is part of life. Whether it be a child, or a parent, or our job, or our spouse, our own health or finances or future, in this life we will all go through some form of dying. The question then is, the only real question, is what we do with our pain.

JESUS

I think of Jesus in the garden on that final night. The hope and promise of resurrection is out there. But, the reality is he knows he must go through the agony of the cross to get there. He has to make a choice.

There are so many parts of the resurrection story that I love. The disciples racing to the tomb. John, in his gospel actually taking the time to point out that he outran Peter, which is comical to me, but perhaps something I would want to write as well. Thomas, who had to "see the nail marks" and put his "hand in his side" before he would believe. Jesus dressed as a gardener. Angels. Guards. A stone rolled away.

MARY

But, there is no character, no person more compelling, more human, more authentic, more open and willing in my opinion than Mary. She is undone by the events of the past couple of days - the bitter pain of the trial and torture of Jesus, the agony and crushing defeat of the cross, the finality and ending of the grave.

And yet, she decides, she gets up early, she says, "I will walk, I will on my own, purposely walk. I will chose to walk to the grave, to the tomb, to the place of agony, death and pain. I will enter in."

She arrives and the stone is rolled away. Jesus is gone. Where have they taken him? And she runs and gets the other disciples. The three of them return and see the empty tomb. But, when the other disciples leave to go home, she stays. And she weeps.

And as she weeps, she bends over and looks in the tomb, and sees two angels. "Woman, why are you crying?"

"They have taken my Lord away and I don't know where they have put him." At this she turned around and saw Jesus standing there, but she did not realize it was Jesus.

"Woman," he said, "why are you crying? Who is it that you are looking for?" What a great question.

Thinking he was the gardener (now that is hilarious), she said, "Sir, if you have carried him away, tell me where you have put him, and I will get him."

Jesus said to her, "Mary."

She turned toward him and cried out, "Rabboni!" (which means teacher).

Jesus spoke one word to her, her name. "Mary." "John." "David." "Bartimaeus." "Lazarus.""Martha." "Peter." "Thomas." "Gae." "Jessi." "Michael." She heard his voice speak that one word and she recognized him immediately.

LORD OF THE UNIVERSE

The Lord of the Universe, the risen Christ, appears first to a woman, a prostitute, someone out of whom he had cast seven demons (Luke 8:3), a sinner, an outcast in her own right, perhaps the one who anointed his feet at the home of Simon in Luke 7, one who had been forgiven much and who loved him deeply.

And that day, her light dawned, her winter changed to spring, her darkness to light, her falling into rising, her "mourning into dancing" (Psalm 30:11), her agony, pain, grief, even death into fullness and life.

James 1:17 says that, "Every good and perfect gift is from above." The Psalms say, that God "satisfies us with good things (Ps 104:28) and that as we delight in him, he gives us the "desires of our heart" (Ps 37:4). What is hard to grasp, and certainly seems counterintuitive to our culture, is that gift, that goodness, is often disguised as a "curse," a sense of dying or death. What can seem like a crushing defeat, can turn into the greatest blessing, the greatest source of light and life, the opening, the well, the "little resurrection" that wakes you up every morning and tells you they are hungry and it's time to eat.

WAFFLES

It is Saturday morning. Gae is out of town. David is watching his iPad. I am cooking waffles. Hootie is cranking on the stereo. The coffee is hot. The butter, warm. The sun is peeking in the window. The Nats are in town. It's a great day for a ride in the park. I begin to dance...

The year is 2015.

Perfect.

Acknowledgments

How in the world do I begin to thank everyone who contributed to this book? The list could be endless. I should start with Gae, who has been my best friend, my confidant, my encouragement, the one who dusted me off and told me to get back in there every time I wanted to give up or quit. She is also the best mom on the planet and to watch her with any of our three kids is an absolute joy.

Jessi and Michael, our two older kids, who continue to make me proud to be their dad, who have helped shape and form David in so many wonderful ways and are both incredible gifts to our family and friends.

Ty Saltzgiver and Howard Freeman who relentlessly edited and spoke into every chapter of this book and created a "dialogue" with me that I will be forever grateful. As Ty said more than once, "it was a labor of love."

Katie Marqkuart who not only leads our Capernaum ministry on the Upper West Side, but is a photographer and took a number of the photos you see in the book including the cover.

Christa Hilt, who is my admin, and also helped edit and format the text, and has helped someone completely blind to social media learn to "post" and to set up a website and tweet and just all around become a #notsonerdyperson.

John Koehler, publisher and friend, who in his own kind

and gentle way, pushed and prodded me to "get 'er done", who really gave me the confidence and encouragement as a first time author to finish, set deadlines, make decisions and would rarely take "no" for an answer.

My Dad who supplied a lot of the pictures of the "Dave," who pulls him non-stop on the tube, and who along with my Mom has been a constant source of wisdom and encouragement since the day David was born.

Gae's parents, Howard and Bettye, who have given David a play place in Texas where cattle roam and coyotes howl and have loved each of us beyond measure from the first day until now.

Our siblings, Nancy and Tom, Mike and Julia, Bob and Carrie who continue to love us and love David and show up everywhere all the time.

Our church, All Angels, at 80th and Broadway on the Upper West Side, who have loved Gae and I beyond measure and continue to be a window into the mystery, greatness and grandeur of Jesus.

National Presbyterian Church in D.C., who was our church for the first 13 years of David's life and continues to be a great source of support and encouragement.

Our house church, or small group, who continues to provide support, love, dinner, fun, laughter, dinner, dessert for Gae and I on this crazy journey of life.

The Capernaum ministry of Young Life who specifically has loved and cared for David. Pam Harmon who leads that part of our mission and has been a lifelong friend to Gae and me, to David and to Michael and Jessi.

The Rebecca School and the Cooke Center Academy, who have provided a family environment for David to learn and to grow, who have helped him mature in so many incredible ways, and really made it possible, at a time when we really weren't sure, for us to stay in the city and raise our boy.

For the greater Young Life family, too many to name, friends, mentors, "family" really who have walked this journey with us, loved us, encouraged us, laughed with us and cried with us every step of the way. We absolutely would not have made it without you.

CPSIA information can be obtained
at www.ICGtesting.com
Printed in the USA
FFOW02n1210210216
21613FF